THE GERMANS:

AN
INDICTMENT OF MY PEOPLE

Deutschland? Aber wo liegt es? Ich weiss das Land nicht
zu finden.
Wo das gelehrte beginnt, hört das politische auf.

~·~·~·~·~·~·~

Germany? But where is it? I cannot find such a country.
Where the culture begins, the political realm ends.

FRIEDRICH VON SCHILLER (1759–1805)

THE
GERMANS:

AN INDICTMENT OF
MY PEOPLE

A Personal History & A Challenge

by

GUDRUN TEMPEL

Translated from the German by Sophie Wilkins

WITH AN INTRODUCTION BY
KAY BOYLE

RANDOM HOUSE NEW YORK

for

ALEXIS FRANCIS-BOEUF

*To shield you from sorrow
was my desire.
To add to your sorrow
has been my fate.
To pray for you
is now my task.
The beginning
after the end;
birth after death:
the eternal law.*

INTRODUCTION

D URING A FIVE-YEAR STAY in Germany, after the close
of World War II, I wrote my first book about that country. It was a collection of short stories, prefaced by a non-
fiction account of the trial of a man who had been proud
of his title, "The Terror of the Frankfurt Jews." The 1950
trial of this former Storm Trooper who had headed the
Frankfurt office for "The Final Liquidation of the Jewish
Problem," had been prepared entirely by Germans, and
it was conducted by Germans in a German, not an international, court. There, in that Frankfurt courtroom, the
German people brought to trial before a judicial body
and a jury composed of German citizens not one isolated
man but the actual reflection of that other German face
which they themselves abhorred. The title of my book
was *The Smoking Mountain*, taken from Theodor Plievier's great and moving novel, *Stalingrad*. In his novel,
Plievier wrote that because the military organization had

outstripped all other departments of Germany's social structure, over and over through history the workman had had to leave his work, the priest his parish, the teacher his pupils, the tiller his soil, and the German people had ceased to exist as a people and become nothing but fuel for a monstrous smoking mountain, the individual nothing but "wood, peat, fuel oil, and, finally, a black flake spewed up out of the flames."

Despite his name, Theodor Plievier was not a Frenchman. He was Germany's greatest post-war writer. And this is a curious thing to be noted about the Germans: however bitter may be the condemnation an outsider voices, however his whole being may recoil from the horror of recent German history, a German will have voiced an even more bitter condemnation, and a German will have recoiled in even greater anguish and renunciation from the spectacle of his own countrymen. Gudrun Tempel, herself chaotically German, cries out on every page of this book against the Germans, just as the greatest German philosophers and poets for decades wrung their disavowal of the German people from the depths of their own commitment to that people. Listen to Nietzsche complaining that the Germans are "more contradictory, more unknown, more incalculable . . . more terrifying than other people are to themselves," while offering in himself the tragic figure of man divided, unable to comprehend and judge himself because unable to see himself in his entirety. But it is Heine who gives us perhaps the most clearly delineated example of divided German man, split and scarred by his own complexity and pain. "German and Jew, patriot and Francophile,"

David Daiches has described him, "sentimentalist and ironist, radical and hater of the organized left, Christian convert and passionate defender of Israel, charlatan and martyr, lyrical poet and journalist, lover of life and perpetual self-torturer—his haunting figure looms out of the mists of social and ideological conflict in early nineteenth-century Europe to appear as the epitome of all the problems that face sensitive man today." Although I do not want to compare Gudrun Tempel with these German writers of stature, her belief is akin to theirs that the German must discover in himself, and consciously put to use, "in a state of inward independence," the possibilities of his German-ness.

Frederick the Great of Prussia is another leading figure in the age-long drama of German duality. In the history of this unbalanced eighteenth-century delinquent one finds the same paradox of condemnation of and commitment to the German people. In his twenties, Frederick sought to give his life a shape and a destination by usurping the identity of Voltaire. This created a witty, sophisticated, French-speaking personality which produced, among other works, Frederick the Great's *Anti-Machiavelli*, a book denouncing war. But, parallel with this alien identity, Frederick established on the battlefields of Central Europe a totally Prussian, German-speaking military figure which bore his name. This second man engaged in ceaseless military conquest, and ultimately created a supreme Prussian state, in which were laid the foundations of the aggressive, militarily-dominated Germany of our time. And in our time is the monstrous example of divided man in the person of

Heinrich Himmler who, during the Nazi régime, declared that not only must the enemy be conquered, but also exterminated, and yet who is said to have fainted when brought face to face with the horror of this extermination.

Explanations are easy to find as to what made Frederick all he was and all he was not. His father had beaten him consistently and ferociously. He had been court-martialed because of his attempts to flee from his own country, and placed in solitary confinement. But once in power, he did what all the German rulers before him had done: he turned for salvation to another nationality. To heal the deep split, not only in himself but in the whole German psyche, he did not ask consolation from the German people, or from German literature or philosophy. He turned in passion and frenzy to France, and to one Frenchman in particular, imploring him in verse (and in French verse at that), beseeching him in music of his own composition (that aped the Italian composers of his day), to restore him in his entirety to the community of mankind. But no man can ask of others a restoration that is his concern alone. Gudrun Tempel, deeply troubled by her national heritage, acknowledges this truth in the pages of her book. "The twentieth century has confronted us with immense questions," she writes, "and we must answer them or perish. We must answer them as Germans, too, since that is what we happen to be."

And one asks at this point: "Why have the Germans never sought to save themselves through their own people, on their own soil, without the help of conquered

territories or of men whose history they do not share?"
Revolution has always drawn the Germans irresistibly,
imaginatively, and yet there has never been a successful
German revolt of the weak against the strong. Germans
from every strata of society were fired by the French Revolution, and not merely for the principle of equality
which it stated. It was also that there, just across the
frontier, could be heard the tremendous sound of a people speaking in unison, as the German people has never
been able to speak. The Germans—and Heine among
them—hailed the French Revolution as the awakening
of the world to a new era of freedom. But it was not for
an instant the awakening of the Germans, and the language that the revolutionaries whom they envied spoke
was not the German tongue. That is a heavy burden of
guilt for any nation to bear: the knowledge that grace of
spirit must be dispensed by men living on another soil,
breathing another, clearer air. And this is the burden that
Germany, and the Germans, have continuously chosen
to bear. Perhaps because we have not always remembered this, Hitler, in all his horror, has seemed to be a
unique phenomenon. But he was not unique. He was a
manifestation long sanctioned by historical fact. In his
sham-revolution of the third-rate against the first-rate, he
was responding to the incessant German demand—reduced to its lowest terms, expressed in its vilest form—
that something greater, prouder, something not for a
moment comprehended, relinquish its dignity so that
Germany might be fulfilled. But Germany as "a new
national state" would now be an anachronism, as Miss

Tempel points out. "There is no other country," she writes, "that needs the security of a United Europe more than Germany."

The second book I wrote about Germany was a novel entitled *Generation Without Farewell*. The leading protagonist in that novel is a German newspaperman of the generation that was under twenty when the war began, that is, of Gudrun Tempel's generation. These men and women grew up under the Nazis, but they were too young to have held positions of authority. They are anti-militarists as their fathers never were before them, and they now express a deep resentment against those by whom they were betrayed. They have no faith in the father image, and they question Chancellor Adenauer's judgment in appointing and retaining government ministers who were officially associated with Nazi atrocities. The protagonist of my novel is not a piece of fiction; he is now on the editorial staff of a large right-wing daily, published in the Ruhr, and he wrote me recently: "I think we are the generation that takes Germany's responsibilities with the greatest gravity. We were already maturing when we made our first contact with the democratic way of life, but not mature enough to have been committed to the old régime. We weighed Western democracy—with all its faults—against the Communist system—with all its striking similarities to the Nazi system—and we made our choice. And now we who are in positions of responsibility on newspapers, in classrooms, and in public office, must somehow reach the generation now growing up, because it is told nothing of the past and can have no recollection of that past." It is this that Miss Tempel is saying as well.

And yet, perhaps just because she is German, Miss Tempel has her own disturbing inconsistencies. At one moment she writes that, as a child, she had such "a complex against marching people" that whenever she saw members of the "SS, or HJ, or NSKK, or whatever, marching along the street," she became physically ill and had to be removed from the scene. Two sentences later she is so swept away by the Nazi "atmosphere of jubilation" that we find her marching "willingly with the *Bund Deutscher Mädel,* the Nazi young women's league." On one page she can write with insight that "the Germans are dangerous, not because they are worse or more cruel than other nations, but because within themselves they have no deterrent against evil"; and on another page, with a detachment approaching callousness, she writes that when one's neighbors disappeared during the Nazi times and were never heard of again, one had "no idea of the extent and horror of the persecution" although the concentration camp had become "a dependable ingredient of the daily crop of new jokes." On still another page we are told, however, that "there could be no one left in Germany who could claim he had not witnessed some of the Nazi atrocities."

But the disorganization and chaos of Gudrun Tempel's outcry come, in the end, to seem a portion of its value. Her protest is marvelously lacking in efficiency —that efficiency which has produced the present *Wirtschaftswunder,* the total industrialization of the soul, which will stand forever as a monument to Adenauer's Germany. It is due to this peculiarly German efficiency, Miss Tempel writes, that "we have today . . . a well-ordered, well-oiled society," impeccably neat and clean. "The engine drivers concentrate on their switches and signals," she continues, "and they do not smile . . . [they] may have a load of corpses on their train, or it may be chocolate. It makes no difference, so long as they get there on time." For a German, she points out, need only be efficient in order to win the respect of his fellow countrymen; while in Spain "efficiency counts for nothing without courage"; and "in France, the efficient man must have intellect as well." Miss Tempel, indeed, is so far from winning the respect of the majority of her countrymen that there are those among them who leave the room when she walks in, and others who sought to prevent the publication of her book. She has no place in the efficient mediocrity of the spirit which is now uppermost in Germany, a mediocrity induced and nurtured by Adenauer who, Gudrun Tempel writes, "did nothing to eliminate the enormous confusion after Hitler," and nothing to bring the Germans closer to the "unambiguous solution" which we recognize, with the author of these words, as "a matter of life or death for Germany."

The past is acknowledged through the writing of books. In the past ten years there have not been enough books out of Germany. This one, with its many inconsistencies, should be welcomed, for the author says in it, "All I know is that I, a German, am literally afraid of the Germans, as I would be of anyone who is unsure of himself and does not know where he is going or what he will do when he gets to a crossroad." She confesses she is no political writer, and that she would have preferred "to write poems about butterflies and lake trout" rather than this book. But in the pages of it she has written as well words we have for a long time listened for to come out of Germany. "What had always seemed most pitiable to me, the violent death inflicted by one man on another," she says humbly, "has now become bearable, because it is up to me to make sense of it, to shoulder responsibility."

KAY BOYLE

Rowayton, Connecticut
1962

CONTENTS

:I:

THE
STONE
IN THE
HARPSICHORD

. . . . .

The German character does not yet exist: it has still to come into being; it will have to come to birth sometime, so that it may become, first of all, visible, and honorable in its own eyes. But every birth is painful and violent.

Posthumous Papers
FRIEDRICH NIETZSCHE (1844-1900)

: I :

Bᴏᴛʜ ᴍʏ ᴘᴀʀᴇɴᴛs had been through the First World War before they were twenty-five years old: my mother with the Red Cross, my father in the army. Both were awarded high honors for courage in action, both came back hating the war; but the war had shaped them. They never knew the ripe middle years of life; it was as though the beginning were followed immediately by the end, childhood by the resignation of old age. Destined by their upbringing and social position to lead, to make decisions and act upon them, they "resigned" at the age of twenty-five. They did not know what to make of their experience of war; they had only the numbing realization that all the killing had changed nothing for anyone.

The inflation swallowed both their considerable family fortunes, but my father became a specialist in plastic surgery. He devised, among other things, a new treatment for cancer of the larynx. He could again afford big automobiles, a chauffeur, a large domestic staff, hunting and fishing trips to Ireland. My mother must have been the first woman who ever drove a car alone to Albania.

They worked hard and played hard, like so many of their kind in the Europe and America of the twenties, yet they never seemed really happy or even contented. I think they felt even then that they had wasted their lives, that they had failed because they could not wrest some meaning from the great slaughter of the First World War. They must have known intuitively that the fate of Germany should be *their* concern, not left to the opportunists, the Hitlers.

But in Germany, families like ours do not even consider going into politics. Politics is dirty, an occupation for men who are good for nothing else, for younger sons who will have no inheritance, for black sheep, for those not intelligent or able enough to succeed "normally." Politics is for the second-rate lawyer, for the student who fails to get his degree. To become a member of the German parliament is to attach to one's name one of the least respected titles in the country.

For this attitude, deeply ingrained in my parents and in all their friends, we, their children, have paid dearly.

Once Hitler had come to full power, they were troubled, but felt helpless. This same feeling of helplessness, of exhaustion, this same escape into hard work and hard play prevails among their children today, after the Second World War.

Germany still has no political apparatus which represents the best in the country. What she does have is not so much democratic as mediocre, and the slightest push will topple it. Its framework is being held up, not from within, but from without, and it continues to exist only so long as it does not give offense. So was it then. If the Weimar Republic had been given Marshall Plan aid instead of the Treaty of Versailles, it might still be in existence.

When my mother hopefully joined the Nazi party in 1931 she was not making a political decision; she had never read *Mein Kampf* and she knew nothing about a plan to exterminate the Jews. It was only that the Nazis looked cleaner to her than the other parties, and they promised work for the many millions of unemployed. In this respect our home, Saxony, was harder hit than any other part of Germany. Mother wanted to help the poor, but without getting embroiled in politics, and Hitler promised to straighten everything out nicely by himself. When she grasped the truth, she tried to break with the party. That was in 1934, just when all Germany was making every effort to join, to climb on the band wagon and make sure of not missing out on anything.

I, of course, attended German schools, but we had an English family friend who not only taught us English, but introduced us to her English, and therefore very different, point of view. My secondary school was one of the best girls' schools in Germany, but as such it promptly acquired a super-Nazi as headmaster. Private schools were gradually being suppressed because the government had no direct control over them, and many boarding schools were forced to close down.

Control was sought on all levels. Entrance to a German university depended—as it still does—on passing a comprehensive examination at the end of one's eight years of secondary school. The examination was government-supervised, and expulsion from school, for any reason, automatically closed the doors of all the other schools to the student. This system enabled Hitler to keep any mutinous notions in adolescent heads well under control. Once when I tried to incite a little resistance in school, none of my friends and well-wishers dared lift a finger to help me when I was threatened with expulsion for "pacifist troublemaking." No one was inclined to take any risk that might have such lasting consequences.

What was it like in Germany at the beginning of the Third Reich, at the time the Nazis took power? Three childhood occurrences which I remember clearly may serve as illustrations.

One afternoon I was shocked awake from my nap when a huge stone came hurtling through the window and crashed, with the terrifying sounds of bursting strings, into the harpsichord that stood not far from my bed. Between the trees and bushes of the garden I saw two men scurry away and disappear into the crowd of men and women shuffling past with red banners—tired men with visored caps, women in long, shapeless cardigans down to their hips, some pushing baby carriages or leading children by the hand.

Then there was the morning when I saw our cook leaning out of the kitchen window, listening, with her mouth wide open, to our chauffeur; he was telling her about a body he had just found on the grounds: "I almost fell over him, and him with the knife still in his back." Saxony, with its millions of unemployed, roiled with street battles; Nazis stabbed by Communists, Communists murdered by Nazis: no week went by without killings. Generally they happened at night, and no one knew what was going on. The people were terrified—mortally exhausted after four years of war followed by three years of spiraling inflation, then by over a decade of upheaval that seemed endless.

Another time I was sitting in a doctor's waiting room, looking out of the window. Streams of workers were pouring from the factories back to their slums. It was a lovely, calm evening, with a gentle, sleepy sun going down. Suddenly the tree-lined square outside looked like a pond full of battling pike. I could not distinguish details clearly, but I realize now that I experienced almost physically that violence—translated into motion, carrying everything before it—which attracts people to boxing matches and bullfights. It rippled and burst, then suddenly everything was still. For a moment, before the police cars arrived, there was absolute silence, and perhaps for the first time in my life I began to count. I needed all of my fingers, too, for there were ten men who did not move when the police poked them, almost gently, with their boots, to see if there was any life left in them.

It was a time of near civil war. In such times of crisis it becomes obvious that Germany is still a very young state—one that fifty years ago was still a loose federation of kingdoms and dukedoms—without a true center or capital of its own to this day. Berlin means nothing to a man from the Allgäu. During the twenties, she had been a splendidly cosmopolitan city, but she has never been *the* city that meant to all Germans what Paris means to all Frenchmen, or London to all Englishmen. Saxons would rather go to Prague, Rhinelanders to Paris, Bavarians to Rome.

To this day Germany has not one political institution which functions *as a matter of course*, so firmly rooted that it can survive all national catastrophes, all wars. There is here no belief in the political effectiveness of the individual, as in France, or the political duty of the citizen, as in England. To arouse the energies of the whole nation takes nothing less than a common "enemy," real or imaginary; Germany as a peacetime problem is seen as too complicated by her people to be faced with anything but their resignation. And once the people feel helpless to solve their own problems, anyone who comes along with a plausible panacea can pick up the reins with his left hand. It was not Hitler's personality that appealed to Germans, but the simplicity of his proffered solutions to our problems, after years of bewilderment and frustration.

It was not the Treaty of Versailles that triggered Nazism in Germany. Other countries, other governments have survived other unrealistic, shortsighted treaties in the course of history. The reason people like my parents voted for Hitler—I am not certain, but I think they voted for him in 1933—was that they did not realize they had any *choice*. Perhaps political maturity consists in nothing more than the realization that one has a choice, that governments come and go but the nation remains.

The real reason for two world wars was not the

Kaiser and then the Versailles Peace Treaty, but the belated attempt to forge into reality a nation which had previously existed only in the dreams of poets and junior military officers. The natural historical process whereby a people works out a political form—sometimes painfully, and over a long period of time—within which it can continue to function fulfilled itself in England under Elizabeth I, and in France, at the latest, under Napoleon I, but never occurred in Germany.

It was not a strong England which brought forth Elizabeth I but a desperate one, and Napoleon was the product of a national catastrophe. The disasters of the last fifty years were caused not by the peculiar German character, but by the delayed fruition in Germany of a universal historical process, in a form which had already gone out of fashion everywhere else. For some reason a truly ancient phenomenon may be more readily understood than one contemporary but old-fashioned. The election of Hitler was an old-fashioned answer to a problem that—in any country that needs no crisis or "enemies" to bolster its sense of unity and its faith in itself—could have been solved by an efficient political machine.

My parents were civilized, intelligent, well-educated people who would never have invited Hitler and his cronies to their table. They would have been bored by that half-educated man's solemn pomposities and lack of wit. But, like almost all Germans, they had a certain blind spot. After the debacle of the First World War they did not know what was left of Germany; now they did not know how it was going to continue under the severe economic strain that had marked the twenties. The war and its aftermath had left them drained of energy, confused, with no political reality to return to.

When Germans discuss German affairs among themselves, they talk of Mercedes-Benz or Johann Sebastian Bach, but not of what really makes a country—its people, its government. Yet when a nation loses interest in its government, or loses confidence in its own power to change its government for the better, that nation is lost. The Germans are like the pre-Elizabethan English in their political outlook, in their lack of involvement with their government. Such an attitude can only produce mediocre governments which, if not supported by favorable circumstances, must end in yielding power to a Hitler.

It was no later than 1934-35 that my parents finally realized that Hitler was a madman. My mother said so publicly and, in consequence, was hailed before a party tribunal. But they felt paralyzed by their lack of political experience; how did one go about removing a head of state? They had no idea of how to begin. The educated German's view of political matters is extremely unrealistic; if he is not dreaming of the impossible, he is disgusted by the actual.

For six years after Hitler's seizure of power most Germans seemed to float on a great dream bubble, and people like my parents, who refused to shut their eyes, were denounced as Cassandras and labeled as "outsiders." No one who did not live in Germany between 1933 and the war can imagine the surge of lunacy—beginning at the latest with the 1936 Olympic Games in Berlin—that swept everyone, however reluctant, into an emotional allegiance to Hitler. The Germans then imagined that they *owed* Hitler something, just as they imagine today that they *owe* Adenauer something and, because of that, cannot send him packing.

Most people saw in Hitler—and many still do—the man who brought order out of chaos. He seemed to have put an end to the political killings; what they did not see was that murder had merely been transferred from the street to a less public place. No more stones came flying through German windows. The young graduate engineer, instead of facing unemployment and an uncertain future, found himself with a job and an opportunity for marriage. Since no one really understood politics—which, as I said before, was considered a contemptible business— Hitler appeared to have earned everyone's gratitude—especially the gratitude of the generation which had come, blundering in confusion, out of a lost war into an economic crisis.

Few people realize that Hitler's persecution of the Jews resembles the Elizabethan war in Ireland in at least one respect: like Elizabeth, Hitler needed spoils to reward the faithful and convince the doubters in his own ranks. Almost every Jewish home in our town was taken over by a Nazi party official; this not only kept the official quiet, but bound him more firmly to the Führer with very substantial ties of gratitude. All those frustrated second-rate lawyers, doctors, publishers, and bankers who had imagined their ways blocked by some "closed fraternity of Jews" in the professions, now found openings created for them. (The sociological history of the

Nazis is essentially that of the frustrated middle class: those who under the Kaiser had had no chance to participate in public affairs, yet dared not jeopardize their hopes of getting to the top by turning even a faint "pink"—by taking their fate into their own hands as Social Democrats.) The owner of the second-largest laundry in our town was now able, as his particular spoils, to take over the big state and municipal hospital contracts that had previously been Herr Blumenthal's. All he had had to do was put the party button on his lapel. It then turned out that Blumenthal's big car was also to be had for a song.

Suppose a citizen of Manchester or Chicago were thus tempted in the midst of an economic depression, and told, furthermore, that his former Jewish competitor was safe with relatives in Sydney or New York. How many would refuse to stick the party button on their lapels in such circumstances?

The answer would depend entirely on *the strength of the party out of power* in the House of Commons or the House of Representatives. It is the give and take of debate between the "ins" and the "outs" which allows each person in the country to hope that things in general, and his own affairs in particular, may take a turn for the better. It is this constant, fruitful interparty struggle which forces the government to explain itself and its actions, inducing the private citizen to take part, to take sides, and to think politically.

We in Germany have no true political power forms and no power blocks. Our political world forms a thin veneer above the non-political mass of the people who are still waiting, as always, to be told what to do next.

An obvious example is Adenauer's relationship to his Ministers and the President of the Federal Republic; even Willi Brandt often looks as though he were waiting to be told what to do.

Forceful, intellectually superior Germans shun politics, for they find something lacking in political life which may be found in business or industry—at Krupp or Siemens or Mercedes—an identification of the ruled with the rulers. The German politician who sits forlorn in the usually deserted *Bundestag* these days—where, during the Weimar Republic, he had beer mugs tossed at his head —is likely to feel that he exists in a vacuum, far from and cut off from the significant currents of life in his country.

It is still difficult to find a university professor in Germany with whom one can discuss the Hitler era calmly, thoroughly, and frankly. Two out of three have not yet understood; their feelings are too mixed. Perhaps the Hitler period gave them their professorships, and whatever else a man may forget, he will remember the beginnings of his career. And what followed those beginnings was so involved that no one cares to think about it. The refusal to become implicated in the daily politics of their country is still the characteristic stance among the most intelligent, the best educated of Germans; no one tries to increase understanding to a point where clear communication is possible.

One of the gravest mistakes made by the victors after 1945 was to believe that all those who were officially Nazi party members had been politically active. *Mitläufer* (fellow traveler), the common name for those who were just barely members of the Nazi party, is a precise term for them: literally, they just ran alongside. Today Germany is once more a country of such fellow travelers; this time, happily, of a better kind of régime. It remains, nevertheless, a sinister aspect of life in Germany. It was not the psychopathic headmaster of my school who taught me fear, it was the silence of my friends when I stood up and spoke aloud what I knew they all were thinking.

While the Boy Scouts were dissolved, the unions amalgamated under Nazi control, and the Jews persecuted, Germans discussed hardly any of it, even in their own homes. But then, neither had they discussed Brüning, the post-1918 inflation, or the murder of Rathenau. I knew at least five families of persecuted Social Democrats or Communists all of whose children entered the Hitler Youth as soon as they had reached the minimum age, regardless of the absurdity of their doing so.

In 1933, when Hitler was suddenly upon us, around us, and later, *in* us, there were few who realized what had actually happened, and those few were ignored as cranks. My parents' circle of friends—industrialists, actors, university men, members of the nobility—did not talk about Hitler, even though many had voted for him as a "middle way" between extreme nationalism and the left. To them, the Social Democrats were a crowd of bakers and butchers, beneath notice, without initiative, guts, real energy, or power of their own. Besides, they were socially unacceptable. Hitler, on the other hand, had cleverly played up his "architectural studies," and this made him acceptable to the middle class. How he man-

aged to appeal to the upper classes I have never understood, and yet so many of the otherwise likable, sensible
friends I have among them are still Nazis in some vague
way. Perhaps they were won over by his venomous attacks against the Communists.

Personally, I can remember no public denunciation
of Hitler between 1933 and 1936, but then, I was still
far too young to see things as other than a colorful pag-
eant. I do remember having a complex against marching
people for a time; whenever I saw SA or SS or HJ or
NSKK or whatever marching along the street I got sick
on the spot and had to be spirited away. But on the
whole there was an atmosphere of jubilation predom-
inating everywhere, a sea of banners and torches which
swept my queasiness aside. I helped our maids put in our
windows hundreds of special candles in red cellophane
cups decorated with the swastika, and marched willingly
with the BDM (*Bund Deutscher Mädel*—the Nazi
young women's league).

We youngsters met on Saturdays and marched into
the woods to play. When it rained, we played charades
in an old pigeon loft that was our headquarters. Apart
from some rather vague references to the Führer there
was no political activity as yet in the BDM. For the
time being, there was little difference between us and the
superseded Girl Scouts, though we wore a different uniform. It was not until much later that I understood the
sinister threat that hung over my family in the midst of
all the jubilation. I was told about the denunciation of
my mother, and her trial by a party tribunal. It should
not be forgotten in judging my generation that while

Hitler floated over Germany on his rosy cloud we were still far too young to understand how things were inter-related.

But when the war went into high gear, we were thirteen and fourteen, an age at which, perhaps more than at any later stage in one's life, one begins to observe things critically. Our assessment of Hitler began with the air raids and with Stalingrad. Unlike our elders, we have nothing to thank him for except hardship and misery. That is why I know no one of my own generation who is in any way still a Nazi. We may prefer not to talk about Hitler, but we have no illusions about him.

In contrast to this, the majority of my parents' generation remember Hitler's "good deeds" as his first political actions and, with a somewhat primitive logic, blame others for all the subsequent disasters. To this day they have not understood that he built his *Autobahn* (express highways) with a view to his coming war. Too many in the professions do not realize that the beginnings of their careers and their first prosperity was probably built on the armaments race, or on the dead body of some Jewish colleague. They continue grateful to Hitler. When the evidence of Hitler's atrocities came to light after the war, they did not understand that they had participated in these horrors, however indirectly, by not acting against them. The childlike naïveté with which they today discuss Hitler covers an abyss of doubt. When questioned, they look foolish, like a business executive suddenly aware that he has been observed stealing an apple off a push-cart. It never fails to amaze me how stupid otherwise intelligent Germans can be about Hitler. Within a very few years he demonstrated their utter lack of political acumen, and of course they do not like to admit it. Worst of all: their mental lapse cost more than a few million lives. Does not one have to be a saint or a sage to face such a truth?

In its early stages, Nazism must have seemed a good thing to the average German, and once on the bandwagon to prosperity, no one felt like jumping off onto the dusty road. By the time they sensed that the axle was breaking, there were so many aboard that it was dangerous to jump. And once the war had started, how could one desert *one's country* in its life-and-death struggle? But, could one save one's country by going along to the bitter end, or by turning back while there was still something to be saved? It was easy for me to hate the Nazis and turn my back on the war effort, for I had not yet formed any bonds of allegiance before the seedy side of Nazism turned uppermost for all to see. It was not so simple for the older people.

Between 1934 and 1938 at least the majority of Germans must have been quite satisfied with Hitler. A sense of purpose and direction swept the country, and economic conditions were improving noticeably. People like my father, whose earnings were greater before than after Hitler's advent, were the exception. My family was exceptional in another regard; my grandfather's second wife was a half-Jew. Because he refused to divorce her—thereby saving her life—my grandfather lost his professorship at the Dresden Academy of Arts, even though he was a famous sculptor, and had recently received the Goethe Medal.

This, and many other personal experiences, moved my parents to withdraw completely from social life, and especially from any kind of political activity. My mother, however, still wavered between hope and despair. For weeks she would be convinced that Hitler was mad; but there were lapses when she doubted her own judgment and concluded that he was a genius after all, but saddled with unworthy, treacherous lieutenants who misinterpreted his good intentions.

My sister was for a time a passionate Nazi in the style of Unity Mitford. In 1936, when she was fifteen, she visited England and liberally aired her Nazi views, to the great irritation of our English friends. They told me later that she had been grandiose, and rather a bore. She lost her illusions entirely as she grew up.

My brother, true to the tradition of our family, showed no interest whatever in politics. During the war he served in the navy which was, as far as I know, the least Nazified of all the armed services.

Never for a moment did my parents hesitate to help our Jewish friends; our house was always open to them. But it would not have occurred to either of them that anything might be done against the persecution of the Jews as a whole, that political action might be taken to stop it.

Of one fact I am, however, perfectly sure: the German people had no idea about the *extent* and *horror* of the persecution. It is true that after Hitler had taken the political murders off the street and organized them more efficiently behind closed doors, one's neighbors would sometimes disappear and never be heard from again. And soon the concentration camp became a dependable ingredient of the daily crop of new jokes; but it was rather as a fairy-tale horror, invented to make the flesh creep, than as a conceivable reality. People had isolated glimpses of a wired train here and heard a whispered story there, but they believed these were the result of individual excesses by a few over-zealous super-Nazis. No one I met at the time, including a few anti-Nazis, knew of any organized extermination of *millions* of people, or of any such plans.

The school I went to was renamed for Karin Göring. My troubles there began one day when I was about eleven. During a Hitler's Birthday celebration in the auditorium, a Jewish girl, Lore Wassermann, did not raise her right arm during the Horst Wessel Song, nor did she sing with the rest of us. Someone informed against her and, because I had stood next to her, I was summoned to the headmaster's office. From sheer pigheadedness—I did not have political views at eleven—I lied, insisting that she *had* sung and, for the sake of plausibility, freely added that she had sung badly out of tune at that. The girl was not expelled, but I had attracted the headmaster's attention, and he did not forget.

Like so many other eminent Nazis, this headmaster had previously been a failure in his profession and a bit of a crook. He had bilked the parents of his private pupils by charging fees for lessons he never gave, and had been expelled from the Teachers' Guild. As a supporter of Hitler he was appointed headmaster of the school which had justly fired him. He spent his vacations as relief officer for the commandants of concentration camps!

The point of this story is that during the whole time under Hitler every world, even the little world of our schools, was split into two parts. The true face of Nazism was often so distorted, perverse, and sinister, that the Germans, whenever they had a momentary glimpse of it, refused to believe in its reality. Every German must have seen *some* evidence of the horrible truth, at one time or another, but his head and his heart refused to fit these glimpses into a self-explanatory pattern, even though that pattern had been prefigured by the very character of the Nazi movement. For those who intuitively sensed the destructive nature of Nazism there remained only a life of near-isolation. Many Germans were disturbed by the outbreaks against the Jewish shops and the burnings of the synagogues, but their feelings were those of the average American when he hears of Little Rock or of the Ku Klux Klan, or those of an Englishman when he reads in his newspaper about race riots in South Africa.

The politically untrained and uninterested judge the life of a country by a layer of surface appearances as thin as an apple skin. It may be that the whole apple is rotten to the core while the brown spot on the surface is no bigger than the head of a pin, and another apple with a spotty, bumpy skin may be sound through and through.

Most Germans enjoyed life under Hitler until the

war, and since they had not taken part in politics previously, they never missed the political choices that, one by one, were being taken from them. The apple looked particularly splendid during the Olympic Games of 1936; hardly anyone in Germany could feel tempted to break it open for the dubious reward of discovering the rottenness inside.

Hitler contrived to make every German feel important in some way. The average German is by nature very unsure of himself and of his role in the world. Everyone was therefore deeply gratified by the illusion of individual significance conferred upon him in his role of farmer, fisherman, stoker, long-distance runner, at the great rallies in Nuremberg, at the Bückeberg, or at some great dockyard. One would see a thousand and one organizations, each in its special uniform, and there were always magnificent "circuses."

There was some facet to attract nearly everyone. My father, a most retiring sort of man and usually deeply suspicious of anything done by Hitler, had tears of joy in his eyes when the long-desired *Anschluss*—Austria's "joining" of the Reich—was announced. He had not the faintest notion of the means by which this had been brought about. How could he? Ours was a country without a free press, without a parliamentary opposition to ask disagreeable questions. He simply loved the Austrians and had never quite understood the need for a border at all.

If you tell the mother of a whore what her daughter is doing, she will probably deny it because it is something she cannot face, and she will hate you for telling her.

This precisely describes the situation of the Germans under Hitler—at least until the days of Stalingrad. When the mother sees her daughter kneeling in church, or when the German sees the "good deeds" of his Führer, both forget everything else.

My headmaster, Dr. Horbach, looked so impressive in his uniform, he was so energetic, so efficient, so neat, so punctual that no one could possibly think of him as anything but the very model of an excellent headmaster. He could, therefore, pursue his prey to the kill without fear that anyone might interfere. His prey happened to be blond girls, especially those who resisted his wishes. He had been married to three blond women, one after the other, all of whom had mysteriously committed suicide. There are, to be sure, pathological cases among schoolmasters all over the world. The significance of this particular case lies in the way in which it was entangled with politics, and in the fact that in an outwardly orderly, lawful state there was no possibility of redress.

The fact that my father sent a monthly check to my grandfather—who after losing his professorship was not even allowed to continue his sculpting privately—sufficed to place me on a special list. For a time I was saved from expulsion by my prize-winning essays, ski championships, and medals for fencing and horseback riding. My picture appeared in the local papers, and the school was proud of me. But from that day when at age eleven I had shielded Lore Wassermann, there was a cross after my name on every list circulating through the school.

When the headmaster canceled our traditional Christmas singing, on the grounds that Christ was a

Jew, I defied him by collecting names on a petition, and the interdict was lifted for two years. As long as I was an outstanding student and kept collecting those sports prizes, he had to be content with an occasional summons to his office to tell me that my parents were swine because they continued to support my grandfather. I could not transfer to another school, or get an education elsewhere; this was his power over me. When he challenged me to become a leader of the BDM, I refused on the grounds of poor health and I had to bring him a medical certificate to prove it.

Then the struggle between us sharpened. He began to interrogate me systematically, at first once a month, then almost daily, calling me out of class in person or sending the porter for me. By the time I was just over fourteen he could see that I was breaking down and he intensified the torture. When we were sent to farms during the summer vacation, to help with the harvesting for the war effort, I was of course assigned to the worst place; my petitions for a transfer were ignored.

Every morning at 4 A.M. we drove out to the fields in the dark and we gathered rocks. Every night at 10 P.M. I was on duty, cooking potatoes. Once I fainted from exhaustion. Afterward I telephoned to my mother and she went to the headmaster. When she called back, she was dissolved in tears. He had threatened to send her and my father to a concentration camp if I fell ill or left the farm—and we all knew that he meant it.

Back at school in the fall, I wanted only to die; within six months my grades dropped from the top of the class to the bottom. In class I would sit as if paralyzed, waiting for the headmaster's steps outside in the corridor, his brisk entrance, the shout of "Heil Hitler!" which greeted him from the class, then the long walk to his office, the wait under the hideous picture of Hitler in a steel helmet—a widely distributed glorification of Hitler as the Unknown Soldier of World War I, which made me shudder.

In many respects Dr. Horbach was the Eichmann type—there is a distinctive Eichmann type, and not only in Germany. He carefully took down in shorthand every word I uttered, writing on large sheets of paper, sometimes underlining with a large wooden ruler engraved with the words "Blood and Honor." If it had not been so genuinely menacing it might have been a farce: a twentieth-century witch hunt against an ordinary school girl shaking under the constant threat that her parents would be killed.

What particularly stoked the headmaster's fury was that I was close to being the ideal type of born leader believed in by so many besides Boy Scouts, militarists, and Nazis. I was physically hardy, resourceful in danger, a winner at sports, a good organizer, and all the rest of it. In addition, I had something of the utmost importance to the Nazis—golden blond hair and a narrow, fine-boned "Aryan" face. What, then, was wrong with me?

I hate being organized, relegated, ordered about— and I am a clown by nature. I cannot help laughing at the absurd, no matter how threatening the context. This trait may strike some as devilish, but for me it means stealing a glance at heaven while I am passing through hell. Yet to laugh or even smile at a person who is pro-

posing to kill you is an unforgivable affront; you are supposed to shake visibly in your shoes. There was something
in the nature of the true Nazi which did not tolerate being laughed at. There he sat, this Dr. Horbach, always
dressed in boots and SS uniform, wearing spurs—of all
things, when I knew that he had never sat on a horse in
his life. The man was a farce, in the same sense in which
we all know today that Eichmann was a farce—a mediocre, overly tidy, middling, bureaucratic intelligence, a
genuine nobody. But this nobody had power over my life
and over the lives of my family, and he enjoyed playing
with it.

Outside in the corridors the girls laughed and chat-
tered. The bell rang for recess, and then rang again for
the return to classes. Outside the windows the blossoms
on the horse chestnuts blazed white and red in the sun.
The sinister side of Nazism was so absurd against this
background that no one could have believed in its reality.
My struggle with the headmaster was known to the
whole school, but no one could take it really seriously,
least of all myself at this moment. When Dr. Horbach
told me what fine children I would bear for the Führer, I
couldn't help retorting that I would like to marry a coal-
black Negro. Horbach's face turned pale with rage.

On another occasion he suggested that I leave my
parents, since they were obviously "unfit to bring up children at all. They are completely weak and degenerate."

Still another time, having just returned from one of
his stints as concentration camp commandant, he said
casually, "I broke the record."

.   .   .

When it became obvious to my mother and me that I could no longer bear the strain, we went to the Ministry of Education. A high-ranking woman official listened horrified to our story and, picking up the receiver to speak to the Minister himself, turned to us for a final check: "What did you say his name was?" "Horbach," said my mother, "Dr. Armin Horbach." The official's face turned to stone. "I am sorry," she said, got up and showed us to the door. "You must be mistaken."

And so the day came when, during my interview with Horbach, I broke down completely. In a last gesture, trying for a glimpse of the sky, I looked out of the window at the horse chestnut trees—and burst out laughing. That was the end. With two strides Dr. Horbach came from behind his big desk and began to strangle me. Perhaps I screamed—I can't remember—for suddenly our hunchbacked school secretary stood at the door. Horbach released me. I left that room and the school.

Shortly thereafter my parents received a letter telling them I had been expelled, and that I was unworthy of serving the Führer in the BDM or the Labor Service (the year of compulsory labor that followed graduation). After this, people often avoided being seen with me. No one, not even my mother, quite believed everything I had told them—until after one day in 1953.

That day an English friend and I fell into conversation with a stranger on the train to Rotterdam. We discovered that we had lived not far from each other in Saxony. He said that throughout the war he had been in a concentration camp and had nearly died there. Since he was not a Jew, I asked him why.

"Well, you'll never believe this," he began. "The headmaster of the school my daughter attended was an SS officer. He kept calling her in for a kind of interrogation. My daughter is a light blond, and incredibly pigheaded. We finally became so uneasy about it that we sent her off to an aunt in Holland. Then they came and picked me up."

My English friend had been listening to him with mounting amazement—she knew *my* story. Suddenly she shouted: "And his name was Horbach!"

"How did *you* know that?" he said.

When I explained, he was almost beside himself with relief.

"You know, I thought so often I would go out of my mind. You see, no one believed me, and often I thought I must have dreamed the whole thing; yet I *knew* it really happened."

I told him then that Dr. Horbach had been shot by the Russians. As the train entered the Rotterdam station, where his wife was waiting for him, he leaned out of the window and shouted to her joyfully, "He is dead, he is dead! Horbach is dead!"

Only now the story became a nightmare for me, which it took years to shake off. I had managed to force it out of my memory as a cruel, improbable fantasy, but now, once more, I knew that it had all really happened to me.

This is how I learned something in my schooldays which most people do not find out until later in life. I learned that the worst nightmares take place just under the skin of that shiny, sound-looking apple, and that even intelligent people, those who *are able* to see the living and dying that go on underneath that surface, refuse to take cognizance of it. For if they did, it might mean having to *do something about it*.

In retrospect, I would say that the greatest failure of that period occurred among the university-educated classes, including the professors. In Germany, these are holders of civil service positions, dependent on the Minister of Education for their appointments and promotions. That which frightened me most was not Nazism itself—I had never been taught to respect the types that represented it, the Horbachs, Leys, Goebbels, and Mutschmanns, our own "King of Saxony"—but the lack of logic among those who had been trained to think, and their total lack of courage. For example, *only one* out of a dozen neurologists—most of them heads of university hospitals—*refused* to take part in the so-called mercy killings. The way in which the medical profession—among others—looked on passively while many of its members were being persecuted was disgraceful. And how many jurists stood up against the twisting and uprooting of one basic legal principle after another? My teachers, all Ph.D.'s, completely agreed with me when, joking with all the cockiness of my fourteen years, I ripped apart *Mein Kampf*, which they had to read aloud to us. "You are nothing, your nation is everything!" Aha, then my nation is a sum of nothings? Yet none of them would risk his pension rights by standing up for me. This is why I still think that pensions and the state monopoly of education can be the seeds of evil.

If the majority of educated Germans had merely kept their eyes open—which they sedulously avoided doing—they could not have failed to see the catastrophe into which Hitler was leading them. What particularly embitters us, the generation that suffered the brunt of that catastrophe, is not only that Hitler was allowed to seize power, and all that happened in consequence; what galls us is that to criticize today the atmosphere and the conditions that made Hitler possible is to be labeled a Communist!

It is not because the preceding generation was "evil" or took part in atrocities—only a small percentage did so —that we feel as we do. We are bitter because they refused to take responsibility for anything beyond their own four walls. And this refusal to look Hitler straight in the face was most prevalent among those who ought to have known better by virtue of their education.

Why did the Social Democrats fail in 1933, and why are they failing again today? I am not certain, but then I do not know much about political parties in general. I cannot remember a time in my life when a party system really functioned in Germany, and after the degrading beer-mug fights in the *Reichstag*, before Hitler—I was seven when they occurred—we had no effective opposition party. Indeed, in all of our history, we can never be said to have had an opposition party which functioned at all. The present opposition party in Germany, as far as one can gauge this from within the country, is more of a comic spectacle than a power in our political life. The smaller parties leap from one extreme to another, so that it is difficult to judge their real intentions.

Perhaps one reason for the political apathy among the German people is that again everyone feels, "After all, we have no choice anyway, so why bother to think about it?" "Our policy is made in Washington," they say, and the presidential election in the United States aroused an interest, a discussion, and an emotional participation far beyond anything stirred up by any of our own parliamentary elections. We feel that our lives, our happiness, our peace, all depend on Mr. Kennedy's decisions no matter who may be in charge at Bonn. All the energies, the abilities, even the sense of risk and adventure that normally go into the political life of a democratic country, are, with us, absorbed by economic enterprises. Our best brains are not on the university faculties, where they would soon be frustrated, or in politics, but in trade and industry.

The reoccupation of the Rhineland, the Olympic Games, the *Autobahnen*, and the union with Austria were the high points of the Nazi régime. But after the Austrian *Anschluss*, the German people wanted to settle down to enjoy full employment and the amenities that Hitler had promised: the *Volkswagen*, the Strength-Through-Joy cruises, and others. It was, after all, the first period of peace and hope since 1914. The greater proportion of the population probably believed quite honestly that the Nazi party would simply become superfluous one day, that its excesses would end, that Hitler's revolution was now complete. Most of the Jews, they liked to think, had found jobs with their relatives in New York. No one wanted war, and only when the people sensed that Hitler was driving them into war did they begin to resent him—not all of them, but a growing number.

We were impelled, however, by the seemingly perennial German dread of encirclement by real or imaginary enemies. As did everyone else, I grew up with this dread. The friendliness of the French and English which we sometimes experience today is something new to us. Germans, who have for so long been treated as outsiders, rejoice in the thought that now they have at last been accepted into the European family. A German who finds himself unpopular abroad, however personal the reasons for his unpopularity may be, instantly and automatically believes that he is disliked because he is a German. Such an idea would never occur to an Englishman.

Between 1936 and 1939 Hitler used all of his suggestive powers to instill into the Germans a deep fear of their neighbors. During the First World War, millions of German soldiers had discovered that the English and the French were like themselves, and that they too longed for peace above everything. The ingredient that makes Germans such good and enthusiastic soldiers is *not* their greater love of war; it is simply that they are thoroughly *accustomed to being told what to do*, and the army does tell them.

The last days before the outbreak of the war are particularly vivid in my memory. Except for the handful of super-Nazis in each town who celebrated with champagne and festive noises, the people were in very low spirits. There was a great, sad silence. Even though everyone, after listening to Hitler's shrill outbursts on the radio, had feared that war would come, nevertheless, the actuality of war burst upon us—paradoxically—unexpectedly. Most people did not identify themselves with "the bloody life-and-death struggle" until the mass bombardments of German cities began, and then, as is only human, few were willing to remember that this terror also stemmed from Hitler. On the contrary, they concluded that apparently Hitler had been right all along: the world did mean to destroy us. The massive bombardments of the cities aborted any real chance of an uprising against Hitler.

The early victories, in Poland, brought a sense of relief rather than of triumph. Most people probably thought, "Now it's all over, thank God." I believe that rationing eased up a bit. It is possible that others may have felt as did my mother, watching the newsreels of the Stukas as they dived, screaming, at refugees—but no one else got up and left the theater, as we did. After all, who gets up nowadays when he sees a mother with a child, running, stumbling, falling, while diving planes loose their machine-gun fire? Since then, we have all become guilty by being bystanders.

One of my ineradicable memories is the sound of Hitler's voice between and during pictures of smoking villages leveled almost to the ground, dead horses with bellies bloated in the sun, soldiers without heads, without faces. What spake Hitler? He was quoting some martial verses: "With men and horses in that hour, The Lord destroyed them and their power!"

Was this little man with the funny mustache the Lord?

The faces of the Polish refugees in that newsreel, as they moved past the marching German troops, bore an expression not only of fear but of resistance which I knew I would never forget. When I talked with my mother about what we had seen, she said, "I feel the same way. I always see myself running, with someone shooting, and then I imagine that it is *they* who are shooting at us and *we* who are running away. It would hurt us just as much as it hurts them now. And that is why it hurts us already. For it is all the same, whoever it is, when a mother is running with her child."

My parents' resistance to Hitler was not political, but humane, personal: a direct, emotional repudiation of that part of history to which they had been witnesses and of which Hitler was the prime mover. This was virtually the only kind of German resistance then; of course, it accomplished nothing.

Germany was not fully prepared for the war, neither subjectively nor practically, as official documents have since proved. She was bristling with neither weapons nor enthusiasm. Even so, most Germans felt the transition from peace to war chiefly through blackouts and rationing. Our losses in Poland were minor; the bloody part of the campaign was behind us by Christmas, 1939. Our military occupation of most of the European continent advanced so quickly, and again with such slight losses to the German army, that people soon ceased to speak of battles. They spoke instead of Paris perfumes and silver-fox capes from Norway. The only question people did ask themselves was: "Where is all this leading us?"

Hitler's answers to this question were so fantastic that they failed to satisfy his listeners. His rantings about a fabulous Greater German Reich to come left them without a clear image of any sort. Increasingly, they discovered that the Nazi party leaders were a clique of extraordinary egotists with unlimited power, and with this discovery the party lost popularity every day. Power groups which had been dormant during the years of general enrichment and relative Nazi moderation suddenly emerged. But these were not really concerned with resistance, only with getting the largest possible slice of the cake. The men who made up the structure of the state—officials, judges, and the like—which had been taken over almost intact by Hitler, now began to chafe under chronic Nazi interference; they were becoming aware of the party's total lack of respect for the law and order for which they stood. The rivalries among the various branches of the armed forces are too well known for comment here. In addition, the conflicts between the army and the party, and the party's own military arm, the SS, sometimes reached insane proportions. Industry, always a powerful force in Germany, began to complain that things were organized poorly and managed worse.

That was all, however. What may have looked like resistance to Hitler was nearly always no more than an expression of injured pride. Each group felt it had not been sufficiently consulted, treated with due respect; each was certain it would have managed affairs far more efficiently if only Hitler would have cut out the others. The man in the street often witnessed a grotesque struggle over precedence, as in the old story of the Nibelungs where the question was, who should be first to enter the church, Brünhild or Kriemhild?

In any case, the various power groups objected not that Hitler was doing something *bad*, but that he was doing whatever it was he did *badly*. I cannot remember anyone expressing moral scruples against the military occupation of so many countries, even though some of them had been unquestionably neutral. It was held to be perhaps a rather dangerous overextension of our forces; that was all.

In our family we have a weakness for maps. My mother always had at least one huge map in her room. On this she used to trace my brother's sailings around the world as a naval cadet—he was in service on a training ship under sail—by sticking little pins into the spots where she thought him to be. She kept this up throughout the war. It had a sobering effect on us. We were none too happy to see the whole continent suddenly under German domination—it made the real Germany look very small on the map. We sensed that Hitler was gambling, not planning. His madness was clearly beginning to snowball, and the avalanche could not be long in coming.

But those three or four power groups were worried about other things. The army feared that the party was becoming too powerful, running the hinterland of the occupied countries—and getting the loot. Industry feared the loss of the unique opportunities for aggrandizement they enjoyed—some rash move of Hitler's might turn the walking war into a running war. The party hated

the army for its victories and for having become suddenly indispensable as one of the three pillars upon
which depended Hitler's power, indeed his chance of
survival.

Yet the average German still had a good life. Many
people made more money than before, and the soldiers'
wives often received not only excellent pay but nice par-
cels containing treats they had never been able to afford.
After the first anxiety over the outbreak of the war had
passed, and once it had become apparent that we were
steadily winning, a kind of stuporous complacency pre-
vailed. Even those Germans who did not take much joy
in the first three years of the war did not find it unbearable.

Complacency disappeared with the Russian campaign. Despite the early victories, everyone felt uneasy.
The "decadent" French and all those little countries
were one thing, but gigantic Russia was quite another
matter. Hitler had now achieved what he himself had
made us fear for so long: total encirclement.

The day Hitler announced that German troops had
crossed the Russian border—as always, the news came
on a Sunday—my father wept. My parents now realized
the hopelessness of our position. The Germans have
been afraid of the Russians from the beginning of our
history, not because they are our traditional enemies—
they never were—but because there are so many of them,
their country is so huge and has never been defeated by
a Western power. Now, if we survived the war at all,
there were only two possibilities for us: to be crushed,

sooner or later, by the Nazi machine, drunk with power after a victory over Russia, or to be flattened under the heels of the Russian troops, whom we visualized as something like the hordes of Genghis Khan—which is what finally happened. Whatever came now, victory or defeat, must destroy us. Even the most wildly optimistic never imagined the Russians as possible liberators.

As week after week went by, the mask dropped completely from the face of Nazism. There could be no one left in Germany who could claim he had not witnessed some of the Nazi atrocities.

Unfortunately, many Germans who then wished to turn away from Hitler saw that they were still facing Russia and Bolshevism. Men who had fought only half-heartedly elsewhere, men who had taken part in the Africa campaign as if playing a game of war, now found themselves on the Eastern front in a struggle where the Geneva conventions were no more than scraps of paper. They were engaged now in a ruthless war not only against a nation but against a continent where everything seemed beyond human scale: the rivers, the swamps, the weather, the distances, the numbers of the enemy.

My mother was still faithfully sticking pins into her huge maps, and, at the risk of the death penalty, we listened increasingly to the BBC at night. I know of four people who were hanged for this act of high treason, but after the battle of Stalingrad every one of our close friends listened in.

One conceivable step in a hopeful direction would

have been to come to terms with England. There was the widespread hope that such a peace, with its resultant interior struggle, might lead to a curtailment of the Nazi power. Many Germans who were critical of the régime were now in uniform and carrying guns. A military *coup d'état* in the French manner, with a statesman-like general established as president of the country seemed a possibility. Still, even halfway through the war, most Germans did not understand the true nature of Hitler, and that only his death would open the way to a change.

Now and then I still went skiing for the greater glory of Germany, participated in fencing tournaments, or broke in horses for the army. But the years of struggle with Dr. Horbach, the daily interrogations, threats, and registered letters to my parents, had created a gulf between me and my schoolmates—between me and the girls with whom I had ridden through riverbeds and along field paths, with whom I had gone skiing on the slopes of the Erz Mountains. After I was expelled from school, I was all but completely isolated. Only the few who came up the seven steps of the terrace to stand at the door to my room could be my friends; we could trust each other.

Most of the boys had been drafted by now and the rest were expecting to be called up. There were about ten whom I got to know quite well: sons of industrialists, professors, nobles. They had all been ardent members of the Hitler Youth, enjoying the camping and flag-waving and even the idea of giving-one's-life-for-one's-country. Their parents were probably in the party.

Not one of these friends survived the war—not even the four girls who sometimes visited me.

We used to sit on the little terrace during the summer of 1944; the air was heavy with the scent of our roses. Someone always brought along a bottle of wine or some special treat. Often one of us got up and played some music—not a record, each of us played an instrument. There was a perfect beauty in those evenings, for the war had simplified and strengthened our friendships. There was great strength in those young men; they were gay and full of courage. There was nothing morbid in the way they accepted their fate, although none of them wanted to die for something they recognized as one man's insanity. When they left, they knew that soon, probably in only a few days, they would be killed, and that the war was already lost for Germany. But there was one thing they believed: that the cruel folly of their death would awaken Germany, and that war and killing would be ended once this war and this killing were ended.

The one I knew best, Joachim Dehn, refused to take part in the wholesale reprisals against women and children in Poland. He was downgraded from ensign and assigned to a suicide battalion along with men under life sentences for crimes. He wrote to me then: "These men are at least human beings." On Christmas Eve he took the place of one of his men on patrol behind enemy lines, and did not come back. His many letters reflect perfectly the slow, painful awakening of my generation. This generation, unlike their fathers, made no compromises of any kind.

It is not my business to call to account any Nazi who has meanwhile come to his senses. But it is my business to answer when a Nazi continues to shout the old imbecilic lies—because he survived the war at the expense of my generation. If one of them says today that he never knew of the atrocities committed by the régime, or that he believed them necessary for the salvation of Germany, I can credit that to his stupidity. But what happened at Hitler's *Götterdämmerung* must have opened *everybody's* eyes.

With their loot and their mistresses, the Nazis ran away—not, however, without encouraging boys of fourteen to make a last stand and, incidentally, cover their retreat. *By what right is a single member of the SS still alive today?* Taking them at their own valuation, they fall short by the very fact that they are still alive after the last battle order. After all, their motto was "Faithful Unto Death." How dare they be still alive? Without having changed? Without insight? With the same songs . . .

The bitter truth is that there never really was a Nazi *movement*; we had, all of us, fallen victim to a freak—the most murderous in history. Most of the big Nazis had joined the "movement" because they could expect to profit from it by personal gain and status which were inaccessible to them otherwise. That which made the party so strong before 1933 was that nearly all the old party officials were men and women who had nothing to lose and everything to gain by the "National Socialist Revolution." There was no movement "Faithful Unto Death." Had there been some other promising horse in the race besides Hitler, they would have all put their money on that other horse.

The Germans are dangerous not because of their aggressiveness, their death instinct, their abnormal cruelty, or their military spirit, but because they have power without political knowledge, political interest, or practical political experience.

In a country in which every child has read in his primer the statement: "You are nothing, your nation is everything!" any kind of act can be committed, since obviously the life of the individual does not matter. Anyone who knows how to play with the masses can have them obediently at his feet. Until the Germans insist upon making their own decisions on the most trifling issues as well as on the most important, until they learn to appreciate the potential power in every single individual, until they learn to respect every individual as a unique, irreplaceable being, they will always remain unpredictable. There is no other country that needs the security of a united Europe more than Germany.

Why have we had the *Wirtschaftswunder*, that miraculous economic recovery which is a marvel even to ourselves? For naked survival, our necessity was trade. When American policy and aid had shown the way, all German energies flowed into trade, just as they had previously flowed into a stupendous war effort, not because the Germans believed in war, but because Hitler had shown the way. The heart of the German people is not really in either of these "miracles."

Where then is it?

I do not know. All I know is that I, a German, am literally afraid of the Germans, as I would be of anyone who is unsure of himself and does not know where he is going nor what he will do when he gets to a crossroad.

Our present stability is an economic stability, not a political one, and dependent entirely on our "Big Brother" America. In the *Bundestag*, which is often more than half empty, all our problems are brought down to the level of defense against Communism. Our political life and political discussion are free, but nearly dead. That Other Germany is forgotten, except in our polemics, or during those weeks they were building the Wall, or among those whose kin have to live on the other side. Claims to the lost territories are asserted in a routine manner.

What would happen if the industrial chimneys stopped smoking one day? Would they find another Eichmann to tote up the millions of the dead in neat columns, and to be promoted in the name of their God, Efficiency?

The Germans have so many faces, one today, another tomorrow. They identify themselves with whatever happens to come their way. Seldom do they relax into being simply themselves.

A United Europe might make a great difference. We would no longer be either victors or victims, but only equals among equals. Many distinguished Germans who would not go into German politics might go into European politics, where the qualities of their new colleagues would act as a challenge, and permit them to discover which values they truly hold. A United Europe would give them the assurance that they are needed; they would not have to prove it in the manner of Hitler.

The abolition of the European battlefields once and for all would be a task to which most young Germans could give themselves with all their hearts.

It would be something to hope for.

:II:

THE
BORDER

. . . . .

"Oh Germany! Alas!
The wolf is ravishing your flocks
While your shepherds bicker
Over a sack of wool."

HEINRICH VON KLEIST (1777-1811)

:II:

THE FIRST our family ever heard about a border be-tween one part of Germany and another was soon after this border had been determined. A relative of mine was working in the Canaris office in Paris, and somehow she had gotten hold of this vital and secret piece of informa-tion. She showed us a small map on which we saw plainly that Saxony was to be occupied by Soviet troops.

We stared at this map and for a while refused to believe it. Then we held a family conference, with my sister arguing forcefully that we must all move to Bavaria. Despite the rationing and the shortages, a family friend had offered to provide us with two trucks and the neces-sary gasoline, so that we could take the most indispensa-ble of our possessions with us. There was still time.

My parents decided to stay, and as I did not want to leave them, I too stayed. My sister, much wiser than us, left, heartbroken over our shortsightedness. Few Saxons could believe in the Russian occupation until the very moment the Russians entered their towns.

As I write this, sixteen years later, I know that most people in France, England, or Italy—to say nothing of Ireland or Turkey—have never clearly grasped the fact that Saxony has become more or less a part of Soviet Russia. There is, in fact, less liberty today in Dresden than there is in Moscow. We talk so much of Berlin, but the complex issue of Berlin cannot be understood at all if removed from the history of the border as a whole. To speak of the border between East and West Germany today is to raise a troublesome series of historical questions: how serious was the mistake made by the Allies; why was it made; and what are the consequences?

These questions I cannot and will not try to answer, but I do know what the border means, as a great many people elsewhere do not. To understand the problem of Berlin, it is necessary to know the history of this border from Hof to Lübeck, which has cost the lives of so many thousands.

Saxony was once one of the centers of Western civilization. There was Leipzig, with its great publishing houses, its university, its Gewandhaus Orchestra, its Thomas Choir; and there was Dresden, whose name speaks for itself. In 1944 and 1945 it seemed quite impossible to us that all this could be crushed under the hooves of the Russians' little Panje horses, under the power of the political commissars and their hammer-and-sickle.

Throughout the winter and spring of 1944-45, millions were moving from East to West in hope of reaching the English and American troops, and in deadly terror of the Red "army of liberation." For months a never-ending stream of mortally exhausted refugees wound through Saxony—East Prussians, Silesians, Brandenburgers, Mecklenburgers, in coaches, landaus, carts. There were some from the Baltic states who had fought in an underground resistance against the German invasion, but now found themselves fleeing, side by side with their former tormentors, from an even worse occupation.

When I had looked on, in 1940, at the French running along their country roads with children and baby carriages, carrying all they could of their belongings, dodging machine-gun blasts from low-flying planes, and at the Poles straying between the front lines from nowhere to nowhere, I had done so not without a deep feeling of pity—but I had been sitting in an upholstered seat in a motion-picture theater. Now it was happening *to us*, as anticipated, but with such terrifying unanticipated swiftness. I knew that history was being made and I was carrying the little crumpled map in my coat pocket; nevertheless, it was like a dream to see that history marching past my garden, the garden of my childhood. Something told me that this was much more than a battle, much more than a war. There I stood in the sun, on our own street, paralyzed by a feeling that something irrevocable was happening. This would change the face of Europe even more than Hitler's wars had done. Of Hitler we had known, somehow, that he was a nightmare and would pass. This was different. It would last.

After Dresden and Chemnitz were destroyed, we moved into a tiny summer house that we had rented during the war, when restrictions had made it impossible for us to reach one of the hunting preserves we owned near Berlin and in the Erz Mountains. The little house stood in the middle of a field, one of the most easterly points the Americans were to occupy before their withdrawal. The events on this field in the spring of 1945 shed a good deal of light on the Berlin problem of today.

So, in the final days of the war, we found ourselves in that narrow strip of as yet unoccupied Germany toward which rolled the Russian tanks from the East and the American tanks from the West. Without exception, everyone in the village prayed day and night that the Americans might get here first. However, unlike the others in Ottendorf, my family and I knew that even if the Americans came, they might not stay.

As the steady stream of military and civilian vehicles passed our field, going from East to West, I found, in a small wood behind the house, many bundles and suitcases containing uniforms, including a complete general's uniform with the *Ritterkreuz*, one of the war's highest military decorations. They were all fleeing toward the Americans. But they did not neglect to set up a rear guard: Hungarian "volunteers," schoolboys of fourteen, men of the home guard over sixty. The Hungarians lived in dugouts and had small mortars, but no idea of what was going on. There was no one to tell them. My mother implored them to go home. What were they defending, she asked them, and against whom? None of them knew. One night they disappeared, and with much difficulty, we rolled the mortars into a swampy ditch. The next thing the decamping big Nazis, army and SS officers, did was to post the old men and schoolboys on the road, with egg-sized hand grenades and bazookas, which few of them knew how to fire. We asked them what they were supposed to do with their hand grenades, and they said, "We are supposed to warn the defense force." We told them that there was none, and that if they listened carefully they could hear both the Russian and American artillery, left and right. My mother succeeded in sending them home also. We hid the bazookas and the hand grenades under moss and branches of fir in the wood.

The next thing we knew, a rocket-firing tank came up the road and took up a position behind our little house. I crossed the field to see who this might be. It was an SS sergeant major with ten men. I could see by the stripes on his sleeve that he belonged to Hitler's special SS Guards. The men sat in the grass and offered me chocolate and cigarettes. Then, having come from the East, they asked me about the position of the Americans. They wanted to know which way to point their gun. I pleaded with them to stop, since it was no longer of any use to fight, but they, unlike their leaders, had decided to fight it out to the last. They were simple men who had believed in Hitler as a god, and it was clear from their expressions that nothing would change their minds.

But our cottage lay in their line of fire. When we heard the crunch and rattle of the Sherman tanks at the other end of the village, we moved to a cave that held an old, derelict limekiln. The shooting began that night. Soon burning cows came bellowing across the field. We could see several distant farm buildings going up in flames. When the survivors of the SS troops ran out of ammunition, they killed themselves. The next morning —a brilliantly clear spring morning—all was still. Using my father's old field glasses, I could see that the Americans had dug in at one end of the field. A Sherman tank came up the road, found the dead SS men, and returned to the village.

Toward noon, having had nothing to eat for two days, we decided to walk to our house although it was broad daylight. We had barely reached it when American light artillery started firing. One of those shells took off our roof. Now we could only walk back—like the slow-moving target figures at the Dresden Fair's shooting gallery—over the rise of the field and past exploding grenades, to our limekiln. Soon the wind blew from the East, and we could hear the Russians. Ours must have been the last unoccupied field in Germany.

Meanwhile a small group of German civilians had gathered at the limekiln cave. I offered to run to the American lines and ask that we be let through. They advised me to tie a large white handkerchief to the end of a stick, but I refused. The sun was shining; the weather was glorious. As I walked along the country road in a great silence heightened by the sudden trilling of a bird, I forgot, for an instant, about the war. Time stood still; I was all alone in the world, and it was beautiful.

The Americans could see me coming from afar. They climbed out of their trenches and stopped me. There were big smiles all around when I spoke to them in their own language. One told me he was a law student from Chicago, and gave me chewing gum. They took me to their commanding officer who agreed to send a jeep for us.

The Americans stayed in the village almost a week. They knew by this time what was happening to those Germans who came under the Russian occupation. It distressed them to think about it, but they would not discuss it. They did answer a direct question by telling me that they already had orders to leave Saxony to the Russians. One night they went away, leaving behind them a despairing village.

Refugees came from the nearest small town, barely six miles away, and what they told us was so terrifying that my parents sent me off on a last attempt to reach the American lines. Ours was one of those partings where no one expects to see the other alive again.

I did succeed in reaching the Americans, despite being under continuous fire on the way, but they were under strict orders to let no one pass. Thousands of refugees were camped in the fields around Chemnitz, some who had been on the road for weeks and months, coming on foot from East Prussia, Pomerania, Silesia, across the frozen Oder River—to get away from the Russians. They had reached the American lines at last. But it was of no use. Except for troops and Red Cross nurses, not a soul was allowed through. I stayed for several days with a post on one of the side roads: they were glad to have an interpreter. As before, the Americans were troubled about the weeping women and children whom they had to give over to an uncertain fate.

One afternoon, having fallen asleep by the roadside,

I was awakened by rifle fire. Those were guns of victory: Japan had capitulated. Early the next morning a GI smuggled me over to the other side. By this time my mother was already cooking for the Russians, not quite fifteen miles away. In her village, there was no girl who had not been raped.

I was safe now, but I still carried the little map in my pocket. I stayed with friends in Hohenstein-Ernstthal, in a beautiful house high on a hill overlooking the distant blue and silver slopes of the Erz Mountains. When the staff of the American Eighth Army moved into the house, we moved into the gardener's cottage; from there we could see the Americans baking their doughnuts, in a plexiglass mobile bakery. The day the blackout was lifted we were allowed briefly to go back to the house in order to switch on all the lights—for the first time in six years. We even illuminated the swimming pool.

At the first opportunity I cornered a staff officer, pulled out my border map, and asked him point-blank whether they really intended to leave us to the Russians. He was silent, and I knew the answer was yes. The evening before the Americans left Saxony, he came and offered to take my girl friend and me—we were both seventeen—to the border of Saxony: as we call it today, the border of the West. I took a long walk during which I decided to stay and return to my parents. My friend also stayed.

The question was not simply a choice between Americans and Russians; it was also a question of whether I wanted to leave Saxony which I loved above

everything—the fields and rivers, our houses, trees, flow-
ers, my books—I was still so young, and everything mattered so much; the very soil of the country mattered a
great deal to me.

The Americans, with their jeeps and trucks, their
plexiglass doughnut bakery, and their Sherman tanks,
left during the night. At ten o'clock the next morning
we heard singing voices coming up through the town. It
was more than one ally replacing another. It was the dis-
placement of one world by another. The air itself under-
went a subtle change.

They marched and they sang. There were no trucks,
no cars—only horses, horses and little green peasant
carts. The nose of each horse barely missed the back-
board of the preceding cart. Whenever the whole proces-
sion halted, the horses were unhitched and let loose in
the surrounding fields. This made the occupation often
look like a flood: it was all over the place. It was apparent that this army had walked from Moscow to Saxony, and that the horses too must have pulled their little
green carts all the way from Vladivostok or Kiev or
wherever to Hohenstein-Ernstthal. In these marching
men and beasts there was something far more indestruc-
tible than any American tanks and trucks and jeeps.

I said good-bye to my friends, who had moved again
into their big house, and bicycled back to my parents.
Our own house in town was now empty. At first the occupation was still thinly spread; the fighting troops kept
rather closely together in the areas just abandoned by
the Americans. Friends told me which villages to avoid

on the way, and which I could pass through in comparative safety. "The Caucasian regiments are safest," they said. "Always try to make your way through territory held by a Caucasian regiment." This was true. The Caucasians seemed to consider it beneath their dignity to so much as look down from their horses as I rode past.

But this is not a history of the occupation, for that alone would fill a whole book. The Russians showed such extremes of kindness and cruelty that, to tell the story at all, one must tell both sides of it. They were obviously proud of being Russians; I have yet to meet a single Russian who does not worship his *country*. I even met a man from Siberia who wept with homesickness for Siberia. I noticed very soon that they feel trapped in a calamitous deadlock. Their régime has made Russia a powerful nation. It was under this régime that they had resisted the German invasion, and finally defeated their enemies, to be free again. Free?

What is the greatest terror for an animal? To be locked in a cage, to lose the freedom of movement. But the first and most consistent tendency of the Russian régime is to restrict movement. Today, when I want to explain to a Communist why I cannot live at home, in Saxony, I must put it to him in the simplest and strongest terms: "Even if I could get permission to live at home, which I cannot, I cannot live there because I would not be able to take the next train from Chemnitz to Dresden, let alone to Paris or Rome." But the freedom to move is an essential part of life. Even a Russian soldier I knew, who had never really known such freedom, cited the lack of it as a criticism of his own régime. We soon saw that the Russians, the victors, had as little personal freedom as we, the defeated, living under their military occupation.

They lived under the same pressure, in the same fear. Theirs really was a strange world. They could never relax except when drunk, and it was necessary for all to be equally drunk, for a sober person in drunken company is—whether he wills so or no—an observer, a watchdog. Hence they were all drunk, virtually every night, and threatening to shoot us if we did not drink with them. Later, when I lived alone in our house, cooking for thirty to forty Russians, I had to learn to drink without getting drunk. I soon learned how to deceive them.

The characteristics of life in all Russian-controlled countries are evident from the first day of occupation: no movement without permission, and no relaxation except through drink.

By now everyone knows that Communist countries are first of all totalitarian; the Communist ideal, of sharing the wealth equally, comes last in their program. It was not the loss of our property we feared then—or that I fear now, when I think of returning home to Saxony—it is the cage one has to enter. It is not that conditions in Saxony are unbearable; what cannot be borne is the existence of *the border*, the line that may not be crossed.

The border existed from the first day of peace; the American troops brought it invisibly forward, then carried it back again. They brought us freedom after Hitler, and they took it away with them again. The American troops and their generals knew this in 1945. That is what makes the problem of Berlin so painful.

It soon became evident that of all the countries controlled by the Russians, East Germany was to be allowed the least freedom. Warsaw, Prague, Budapest, Bucharest, even Moscow—all are preferable to Dresden. For the East German Communist régime was set up by Germans—not only the handful of German Communists who returned from Russia, but many other Germans as well—and they set to bringing the new totalitarianism to East Germany with such vigor that they often surpassed the Russians in their zeal. They were eager to be more total than anybody else.

The inhabitants of Saxony now began to leave their towns and villages by the thousands. Some felt they could neither stay nor leave: during the early months of the occupation whole families went into the great parks and the town woods and hanged themselves. Sometimes they carried kitchen stools, and almost all wore their Sunday clothes. Others, the moment they believed themselves under surveillance or on some list of those to be persecuted, tried, as they still do today, to cross the border.

The border was at first ill-defined and ill-guarded, but by the fall of 1945 trenches were dug through the fields and along the villages which were now declared to be within the boundary zone. That was the first time I went across. Everything we had owned was gone now, taken by the Russians or confiscated with a scrap of paper or a wave of the hand. My parents still lived in the village. Much had happened that made it necessary for me to leave, so I went with friends to the Harz Mountains, where it was supposed to be easy to "cross over."

We soon learned a basic truth: wherever human beings live in a cage, there are rumors in circulation that the cage will soon be mysteriously opened. The people inside the cage are more nourished by such hearsay than by their daily bread. Today, rumors are making the rounds that Berlin is to be traded for Thuringia —and the Thuringians thrive on them. In 1945 I met Saxons who told me that Eisenhower had been seen in Dresden, and that Schleswig-Holstein would be exchanged for Saxony. Some of the stories sound baroque, beginning, for example: "A woman dressed in white came to the *commandatura* in an American car . . ." Such stories were being invented afresh every day, and are still being invented sixteen years later.

The idea was that if the Western Allies were fighting, as they claimed, for the liberty of the individual, they could not possibly leave us, the Saxons, Thuringians, etc., deprived of ours. They could not leave us in the ditch without putting the lie to their war aims and totally destroying their own image. It did not occur to us that the French and English and Americans had obligations toward their own war-weary people. Neither caged animals nor caged human beings can be expected to be objective. They are obsessed with the desire to get out of their cage.

My first crossing of the border was perhaps the easiest. It was a mass outbreak from a little electrical train in an area in the Harz Mountains for which the English and the Russians had not quite agreed on a definite border. The train was crowded and I stood by the door as we rolled through the countryside; the tracks were parallel to a small road. Suddenly, Russian troops appeared—on foot, on bicycles, on horses, in a truck—and gave chase to the train. Unbeknownst to us, the border had been settled the previous night. The train stopped, a little ahead of the Russians, and everyone scrambled out and ran in the direction of the British occupied zone. Most of those running had children or luggage impeding them, and soon a young man and I reached the road barrier alone, while the others still struggled up the road on the Russian side. Rifle fire broke out behind us, but we could not see what was happening for we had reached the forest and had begun to climb down toward the first British troops I had ever seen. They looked at us but asked no questions. The young man and I reached a big park and I suddenly realized that here was the gate of my sister's boarding school in Vienenburg! I had been here for little visits at tea time. It was a peculiar feeling, to have run across a military border, with people getting shot behind me, and suddenly to find myself in my sister's school.

I was overcome, then, with a second realization—it had to come to everyone who crossed the border from East to West—the realization that each trip, each crossing over, each return, would be a matter of life and death. It would mean deception, walking by night, having another person's passport: always taking chances. To have crossed the border made me a criminal in the eyes of the régime, and nothing could undo my crime. My crime was to have traveled from Dresden to Hamburg to see my brother—without first asking permission.

This is not all, but it is enough. It is a yardstick of the failure of forty-four years of Soviet rule: they find themselves unable to grant man his most essential liberty, the liberty to move, anywhere, at any time, as I can move today, living on the other side of The Border.

Not long ago there was still a hole in the wall, not altogether safe, not altogether comfortable for someone from Saxony or Brandenburg, but still a hole. The other way, the way through the Harz Mountains or Sonneburg or Coburg, was a possibility for young people who could walk, swim, ride a fast horse. But with the introduction of the two-mile plowed-up strip, and the watch towers, this too has become impossible.

There was no postal communication with the Russian zone in 1946. The first news I received of my parents after I had left them was a little note, delivered by hand, saying that they had nothing to eat. I was working in an American tuberculosis hospital and had plenty to eat myself, but I was ill; they kept me going with strychnine injections. It was clear that I had to go back across the border.

A friend came with me, a man of about fifty who had been in the resistance during the war, very tough and very courageous. He was an ideal companion for such an undertaking. We set off for Coburg. I had a knapsack full of food which I could not lift by myself. In Coburg we were supposed to meet our guide, a paid man who took you across or who just took your luggage and disappeared, leaving you between the lines—one never quite knew.

My companion came back from the rendezvous alone; the guide had been shot the previous night and the whole border around Coburg was in a state of special alert. We talked it over; I was set on going. My friend agreed on another try. Rumor had it that we would find another guide in a small village not far away, and we did. After we had paid him, we waited in his small cottage. The night was perfect: drizzle, a slight fog, a sliver of moon.

At midnight we set off, the guide leading, then I, then my friend. Soon, big lumps of moist earth clung to my boots as we crossed freshly plowed fields. I could not see beyond our guide, but I was aware that we were crossing hilly country: up, down, up again. We had instructions to stop moving whenever we heard a sound. We heard two Russian guards on a road slightly above us, and we stood stock still, right in the middle of a bare field. I could all but feel the two horses coming, one from the left, the other from the right. I could see nothing, but from the sound I knew they were fairly small horses, trotting, and they were bound to meet right where we stood.

We must have been plainly visible, but since we did not move we could have been mistaken for willows—at least I clung to that hope. But this comfort did not last. My next thought was that they were bound to hear my heart beating—it was pounding like a kettledrum and ready to burst. The two Russians had slowed their horses to a walking pace. They met about ten yards away from us. They talked, fell silent, talked again, looked around, then turned their horses and trotted away.

Breathing once again, we crossed the road into another field. Eventually we reached the first village on the other side, where we were supposed to rest until about 4:00 A.M. Our guide tapped out the prearranged signal on a farm-house door. Ages passed before the door was opened about two inches. There were excited whispers while we waited in the dark. Then the guide turned to us to say that some Russians had been shot at, and the whole place was under alert. Anyone caught without the local identity card would be shot, as well as any local people who were found hiding such a person. He pointed vaguely into the dark toward another village where we supposedly would be safer, and disappeared forever, as if the night had swallowed him.

My only wish was to be dead. I was carrying a few pounds of March-wet Saxon soil on each of my boots, and I dared not take off my knapsack; it weighed more than I did, and once set down, I never could have lifted it onto my back again. But one never dies when one wants to, and we walked on, found a road leading in the direction toward which our guide had pointed, and continued. After a few minutes we heard a car approach, and my friend pulled me into the ditch which was covered with a thin layer of ice over some three feet of water. I do not know how many times we had to jump into that ditch. Our faces were only inches away from the road on which horses and cars passed in both directions. The stream of traffic continued until, long afterward—I could not tell the time—there was a lull and we trotted on, barely conscious. We felt as if a whole Russian army must have passed us during that night.

Suddenly the strong beam of a flashlight shone straight into our faces. I was sure that this was my end, surer than I had ever been before—even when an automatic had been pointed at my chest. Perhaps I longed for the end to come.

From the darkness we heard the voices of two Germans asking us where we had come from and where we wanted to go. We could hardly believe our luck after such a night as this had been. They told us to wait in a bakery at the edge of the village until dawn, then to make our way to the nearest station by crossing a cemetery. A train was leaving about 7:00 A.M. But we would have to be dry, and cleaner, or we would be arrested there.

We found the bakery and in it two young Germans who had tried to cross the border in the other direction, but had failed. The bakery was a small stone building with an earthen floor; one wall, containing the oven, had long narrow holes in it through which the baker pushed the boards carrying the loaves. There was nothing to sit on but the earthen floor with its puddles. The oven was still warm, and we were dripping from head to foot with the icy water from the ditch. Yet there was no way of reaching the warmth inside those narrow, long holes, and so we spent the next hour looking at it like drowning people watching a raft that they cannot reach go drifting by. The unalterableness of it made me think of Greek tragedy, which I had never understood. Stand-

ing there, freezing slowly to death, with all that warmth
an arm's length away and yet beyond reach, I did not
understand Greek tragedy any better, but I could *feel* it.
All four of us were too exhausted to talk or think or
move.

After a long time one of the young men came over
and took off my knapsack, the straps of which had worn
through my shoulders almost to the bone. It was full of
American army food: cans of Spam and lard, packets
of chocolate, coffee, sugar, vitamins, even salamis from
one of the hospital officers. If it had been found by one
of the Russian border guards, these supplies would have
sealed our fate.

At dawn we left the bakery and walked up the road
to the station. I came close to fainting when I felt the
two straps of the knapsack on my shoulders again. We
were now further inside the zone and the road was deserted. Soon, a man came up to tell us of searchlights
and a barrier further down the road. We walked on and
up a very long hill. Suddenly, and for the first time in
my life, something inside me snapped. I gave up. I sat
down beside the road and told the others to go on alone.
I told them if all the Russians in the world were coming
I could not and would not move one more inch.

My companions did not know what to do. In the
end the two young men picked up my knapsack and carried it between them. Walking without it was sheer
heaven and I did continue up the hill. We reached the
top, and at a slight bend in the road, two strong searchlights caught us. The two young men threw my knapsack into a hedge that was twice my height, pushed me

and my friend through after it, and continued in the light, marching toward the barrier. For the best part of two hours my companion and I tried to get through that big thorny hedge, with the searchlights still waiting to catch us. We had no choice. When we cleared the hedge to the other side we were in the cemetery near the station, but the train had already gone.

The Russians had ripped up one out of every pair of railway tracks in Saxony and in every other place they occupied. The next train would be coming through during the early afternoon—perhaps, and perhaps not. Fortunately, cemeteries are equipped with water taps, and we were able to clean ourselves and wash away the blood from the long scratches dealt us by the hedge.

Late the next evening I reached Ottendorf in a snow storm. At the tiny station, my mother was waiting, and when I asked her for whom she waited, she said, "For you." It had been almost three weeks since she had sent the little note by an unknown man whose crossing like ours had been subject to chance. But my mother said she had known I was coming—and on that particular evening. She had even brought a little cart for the knapsack, because we still had to walk another four miles to the other end of the village.

From the moment I saw my mother's face, I knew that there was no hope for my father. They had lived on potato peels and carrot scrapings for too long. My father was still conscious and recognized me. He saw all the wonderful food I piled on a table, but he knew, as a doctor, that he would taste none of it. I was too late by about five days.

. . .

My mother continued to live in Saxony until 1949, and I crossed the border several times to bring her food or, as in the summer of 1948, to work her quota in the open-air mines, so that she could get her coal. Sometimes I walked through the woods or swam a river. Once I rode horseback across the border with a friend, each of us leading a second horse, all thoroughbreds, with which she hoped to found a new life for herself in the West. We were shot at and my friend later died from her wounds. The horses went on to win many races.

Things grew more difficult each time, not only because of the new watchtowers and the two-mile plowed strip; to be caught in Dresden or Chemnitz or Ottendorf had become much more dangerous—the East wanted to keep its young people.

In the spring of 1949 my mother had to register. Because of her time in the Red Cross during the First World War she was a qualified specialist in combating epidemics, and she was in danger of being sent without warning to Mongolia or God knew where, in spite of her age. She sent me an SOS. Because of her age and ill health we decided she would have to come "legitimately" by train, with a false identity card. My mother, whom I had never seen afraid of anything, was by now worn out and terrified. The mere existence of The Border, of that cage—the knowledge that one was immobilized—was enough to wear one out.

I took identity cards from friends who vaguely resembled us, got tickets for the Leipzig Fair, and spent hours imitating my friend's signatures. I would have to go through the border station twice for two entry visas, one for my mother. I tried out scarves and make-up. I had to have two coats, two pairs of shoes, two of everything, since I would have to appear as two different people; the public toilet would be my dressing room.

I cannot now remember all the details, but I managed somehow. My worst moment came when one of the Eastern police came up to me, stared at me, then went away. When I had passed the control station hut he came up again, addressed me by my real name, and asked how my father was. The man had clearly recognized me; there was no use in lying. I told him about my father's end four years earlier, and that I had come to fetch my mother. The policeman told me that he had been a gamekeeper and had trained some of our dogs. Apparently at one time my father had done him a good turn. He whispered, "You are right to fetch your mother," and disappeared back inside the hut.

A visa for the Leipzig Fair does not entitle one to go to Dresden, to Halle, or to Chemnitz; one needs a special permit for that. How was I to get a train ticket to Ottendorf, not to mention a permit? We made it somehow, changing little local trains every ten miles or so.

On the way out we spent one last night in Leipzig, in the apartment of friends. My mother was very tired and stayed in to rest, while I went to the Thomas Church across the street. Professor Ramin was rehearsing the Thomas Choir in Bach cantatas. Quite a number of my childhood friends had been Thomas choristers, pupils of that boarding school of which J. S. Bach had been a teacher, and I knew Ramin well. We chatted, and, during a break, I gave all the chocolate I still had to the boys. When they continued their rehearsal I walked up to a gallery and sat down to listen. We had often joked that the choir would sing at my wedding, my answer being that I would marry solely to hear the choir sing.

When the rehearsal ended, Ramin turned around: they were going to sing something for me. It was not for my wedding, it was a farewell from all I had loved and known; Ramin knew it, the dark, empty church knew it, and the boys must have guessed it. Their singing was much more than beautiful, and very strange. When it had ended something had left me forever, and I realized only much later what it was: innocence. I felt as though I knew everything that was to be known.

Mother and I went on to Munich in one of those special Leipzig Fair trains. In those days the line did not carry you over the border. Everyone had to get out of the train, go by bus to the control hut, take another bus to the other end of the track, and then back into the train. In a way, this gave us our one chance. We waited with the others outside the hut as it began first to rain, then to hail. My mother was full of apprehension. Again and again individuals and small groups were led out and away from the hut by Eastern police: caught. They had been caught in the act of traveling from Leipzig to Munich—about the same trip as from Chiswick to Oxford, or from New York City to Buffalo. They had had the misfortune of living on the wrong side of the border when it was determined in 1944.

My mother felt quite ill; it was bitter cold, and she

had not had enough time to practice the signature she would have to forge inside the hut. We decided that I would again go through twice. My mother would wait until I brought back her identity card with a stamp permitting us to board the bus. In the general muddle caused by the rain and hail we succeeded.

Neither of us has ever been back. It is much easier for me to get a visa for Moscow today than one for Dresden or Ottendorf or the Erz Mountains, where we still in theory own a skiing hut, or for any other place in Saxony. There is no way of finding out what happened to my father's grave. Most of my Saxon friends and relatives are dead, either executed after the attempt on Hitler's life on July 20, 1944, or killed in the Dresden air raids, or by artillery, or suicide, or rape, or disappeared, leaving no trace, during the mass deportations. Those who are alive are in Mexico or Australia.

But no, this is not altogether true. There are still friends in the cage, our maids and charwomen, and Ludwig, our last chauffeur—the people that Khrushchev supposedly likes and fights for. Right beside me are some letters quite as desperate as the note my mother sent me when my father was starving to death. They are not pleading for food, they plead only for freedom, to be let out of the cage. . . .

During the last twenty-three years, hundreds of thousands of people have crossed borders in Europe under circumstances similar to those of my 1946 crossing. It is no longer anything unusual. But the crossings of The Border have been made in peacetime, by people like me—students, women, children. Not criminals, not political refugees, not members of some underground organization, but children bringing food to their starving parents, mothers going to their children. It is not even a border between two countries, but an arbitrary dividing line between neighborhoods that were normally deeply intertwined.

The question of Berlin is not merely a question of two million West Berliners, or of so many square miles of parks and buildings; it is the question of the cage: Berlin would never have become a problem without The Border which has been *a cage* from the hour the Russians set foot in Saxony to this very day.

It is a terrible thing when history steps through one's garden gate to confront one. This has happened to the East Germans even more than to those in the West. What have they learned from their merciless lesson in history? To think? To be on their guard? To remember and understand? It all began so simply. Amidst the music of trumpets and drums, a special announcement, like so many others since the coming of Hitler: "The Führer has ordered the German army to march into Russia."

:III:

THE
GOD
EFFICIENCY

. . . . .

It is a harsh thing to say, and yet I say it, because it is true: I know of no people more torn apart than the Germans. You will see craftsmen, but no human beings; philosophers, but no human beings; priests, but no human beings; masters and servants, young people and settled folk, but no human beings —is it not like a battlefield where hands and arms and broken limbs lie scattered, while the spilled lifeblood drains into the sand?

Hyperion
FRIEDRICH HÖLDERLIN (1770-1843)

: I I I :

THE QUESTION, "What do the Germans believe in?" may be the hardest of any to answer. In trying to answer it I have written and torn up so many pages; I have gone off to Italy and France for perspective, trying to get to the bottom of the problem, trying to formulate what is so resistant to formulation.

There seems to be only one way and one I wanted to avoid: to be ruthlessly honest, at the risk perhaps of being unfair now and then.

When we Germans look back upon the last thirty years we see a vast herd of ostriches: ourselves. We evade the truth more than any other people I know. A brilliant young English historian said in the *Sunday Times,* "The Germans are dangerous." Are they dangerous? Are they anything at all?

Try to reach a German and ask him to stand still so that you can look him in the face. As a non-German, you will find it impossible. Improbable and queer as it may seem, it is impossible even for me, a German. If you asked me to define the German character in one sentence, I would say, "The German is an eternal evader, a dodger." He sidesteps responsibility—hence Hitler's success and Adenauer's incomprehensible durability.

The German has the *illusion* of power and importance. Actually, he has no power because he is guided by systems and signals set in motion outside himself. The German's danger is not that he might lose control of his power but that he cannot and will not lose control. He pays attention to nothing but his signals. He is without any doubt the most servile of all Europeans. He has been drawn with a ruler, measured out with a yardstick. Any humane impulse, even toward himself, tends to be choked off.

I love Germany and, in the strangest way, I love the Germans. They seem pitiable to me, like a man whose heart cannot beat because the arteries are missing. I love them but I cannot live among them, no matter how earnestly and how often I try. There are no bridges between them. They cannot be reached. One may talk with a German, laugh with him, see him weep, and think: There, now! here he is at last, this is Herr M. But Herr M. does not even know himself who he is, where he begins, where he ends. There is nothing definite in him. There is nothing definite in the Germans.

Take the man who wrote in *Der Spiegel* of October 4, 1961: "I was in the SS and I am proud of it. I do not believe in God, I believe only in ourselves." He is a definite person, is he not? Surely he has a distinct outline, a form of his own?

But no, he cannot and he does not have any such thing—or he would be dead. According to his creed, his own standards, he could never have capitulated in 1945.

The Germans were Nazis one day, and ceased to be Nazis the next—now they are democrats. Are they really? Certainly, as much as they ever are anything wholeheartedly—which is never. Even a man like Eichmann has no outline, no form. He was the engineer of an especially powerful engine; he followed his tracks, his signals, his switches.

Is the German ever truly committed, with his whole person?

He is, in one respect only: where efficiency and obedience are involved. Nothing else ever really touches him and his sense of honor. If the German character has legs upon which to stand, these are they. A German who is efficient need not be anything else to be respected and admired by his fellow countrymen. In Ireland, the efficient man who is also a miser is despised. In Spain, efficiency counts for nothing if not complemented by courage; in France, the efficient man must also have intellect. What good is an efficient Englishman who is not also a gentleman—or at least a character? Only in Germany is efficiency sufficient unto itself. My definition is crude, certainly; but how is one to define the lack of something?

Take away efficiency, and what remains of today's German?

Where are all the young Germans, so deeply thoughtful and perplexed, who attended the university with me in 1947?

Still baffled and uncertain, they are swimming along

between the ropes with the new German mark. Each wears an invisible sign around his neck: "Do not disturb." He does not look around. All he does is concentrate on the ropes that guide his nose, wherever they lead. His is a moment-to-moment existence of established stroke and efficient splash, based on faith in the guiding lanes.

Was Hitler efficient? If you believe that Jews are dangerous, then he was very efficient; though, to be sure, there is Israel—perhaps he was not efficient enough. If you think of Russia, he was efficient, since he saw the danger which seems to threaten all of us today. America, England, and France were too decadent to recognize it, and now there is no longer a Hitler guarding them against Communism in the East.

What am I saying? I am repeating verbatim a conversation between two Germans I overheard last night in a restaurant. It is of a kind that might have been heard almost anywhere in the country.

Are you beginning to feel superior? Not so fast: the first Englishman I met in England, a sheep farmer in Sussex, said to me, "But why didn't Hitler kill *all* the Jews?"

Where then is the difference?

That farmer was only one man, and there were others around him who held other views, a great variety of widely differing views. There are those who play golf and have one set of values and others who breed guinea pigs and have another. The world over there are eccentrics—except in Germany. There are extremists; there are cranks; there are the English who stage a sit-down in

Trafalgar Square; in Normandy there are people who barricade a street with plows and throw tomatoes, but offer the tourists the most delicious kinds of cheese gratis. And they smile!

I wish the Germans could learn to smile. For no reason at all, just like that, even to themselves.

But the God Efficiency is a solemn god. You can elude him with the contents of a bottle under your belt, but you cannot smile in his presence.

Now at last we have the Germans in focus, those millions of them who cannot be either Nazis or non-Nazis, for they failed both ways. If we never before understood why they could not be one or the other, we do understand now: they will not face the fact that for once in their lives they were thoroughly inefficient. If they did face it there would be nothing left for them to hang on to; their train would go off its track . . .

Many Germans counter the question: "But you were a Nazi, were you not?" with, "After all, the English invented the concentration camp."

How do the Germans justify themselves? They reason: why be good when no one else is? Why be ashamed of something others have done before us and will do again? As for the millions we killed, others have killed, and raped, and robbed, just as many. Everything is reduced to a simple calculation: if I was ordered to do it, I was right to do it.

So we have today in Germany a well-ordered, well-oiled society, very neat, very clean, very efficient. It calculates, it adds, it subtracts, but it does not reflect. It wears a sign around its neck: *Do not disturb.* The engine drivers concentrate on their switches and signals, and they do not smile. As long as there is no accident it does not matter who orders the signals: Hitler, Adenauer, Kaiser Wilhelm—it is all pretty much the same. There is no hitch, just so long as the machinery functions; the wheels are oiled, and the paint is shiny. The engineers may have a load of corpses on their train, or it may be chocolate. It makes no difference, so long as they get there on time.

The German is inherently no more cruel than other people; everyone has more or less the same instincts. But in the German there is no pull in the other direction to act as a corrective. He is born and brought up in the image of efficiency: efficiency and obedience; not *joie de vivre*, smiles, Nelson's blind eye, *noblesse*, generosity, feeling for the underdog, or mercy for the fellow who is on the outside looking in.

I know of many young Germans who tried to put all those virtues on their shields after the war—this war full of horrors, and followed by more horrors as the concentration camps were opened to the world—then threw them all away again, quietly and secretly. Why?

Because Efficiency excludes the possibility of having a real position, of taking a stand, of inner participation, sympathy. No one in Germany today wants to sympathize with anything. The Germans, the very people who hold the keys to war and peace in their hands, turn their backs on everything that seeks their sympathy, past, present, or future. They have forgotten, or have never learned, that, want it or not, they are involved with the world's problems, in the thick of them, sitting in the same boat with everyone else; they do not see that every day they avoid decisions, do not act, think, debate, say either *yes* or *no* to the past and the future, brings the total catastrophe nearer.

They have not yet answered the questions of their children. The children cannot tell a good man from a bad, a dangerous one; they have never learned how to make that distinction. All they can tell is who is efficient and who is not. That is something that can be measured. When the former SS chief proudly wears his *Ritterkreuz* to an embassy reception, this is an indication, is it not? It is a medal. A medal . . .

:IV:

A FUTURE WITHOUT A PAST?

. . . . .

How seldom I see a face that speaks a firm, decisive language. Most of the faces are so blurred, so lacking in freedom; so much is written on them, but all without assurance, without greatness. Everything is so blurred, so intermingled: in the young there is something of the old, in the healthy, something of the sick.

Briefe eines Zurückgekehrten,
(April 1901)
HUGO VON HOFMANNSTHAL (1874-1929)

:IV:

THE GERMANS in this century have been dealt the most agonizing history lessons imaginable. What have they learned? Do they have any ideas that go beyond the past glories of the *Autobahnen* and the present glories of the latest Mercedes? Will their future political decisions be dictated by emotion, by thought, or by the political gamesmanship at which they are notoriously inept?

For many years the Germans lived in a dream—the sort in which one floats in mid-air, touching neither top nor bottom. We did not have to say *yes* or *no* to anything of importance: neither would have made much difference. Washington and the Old Man in Bonn were taking care of everything nicely. The Berlin airlift was carried on in such a boy-scout spirit that the danger of the situation was hardly recognized. Criminal Nazis were shielded, given their pensions—anything to keep things quiet and avoid raising ugly issues. People often played a game of pot and kettle: when one shouted "Nazi!" the other cried back "Communist!"

Life in Germany continues on the principle that the less said and remembered, the better. Let us not jeopardize the butter on our bread; we have worked hard enough for it.

The German God Efficiency brooks no rival. Also, his cult yields tangible, measurable results, whereas politics is a peculiar game in which the greatest successes are often achieved in secret, and may not even be recognized as such until a half century later. Of course, that is true of the failures, too.

If Germany loses the territory behind the Oder and the Neisse, the ex-, pseudo-, and semi-Nazis will be the first to cite the Geneva Convention and the right of self-determination. The man who will be blamed will not be Hitler, or Ulbricht, but Kennedy, who had the least of all to do with it. Germany will have been "betrayed" once more.

The Germans are playing a dangerous game. They are stuffing themselves with their cake and wondering why they cannot have it, too. For the past ten years they have been fattening on the cake that is the Economic Miracle, the *Wirtschaftswunder*—a cake not earned by their own political efforts but handed to them as a gift by the allies who defeated them. Any thinking person should have known that such "miracles" have their inevitable price.

The headlines in the German newspapers should not read: "Has Kennedy Betrayed Us?" They should read, "Will Concessions Help Us Any Further?" Will concessions help us to remain free? Since we expect the whole world to put supra-national interests above purely national ones, we cannot begin at this late date to run up the banner of nationalism. We have twice been thrown through the door out of world politics. Today we are more vulnerable, more powerless than ever. Do we really want to ask for a third *Götterdämmerung?*— merely to prove that we exist? Is it only idle chatter that keeps cropping up everywhere or is it like the wind-borne seed of the deadly fly agaric mushroom? Is Adenauer playing a game when he says, "Never an Oder-Neisse border!"—he, who in the 'twenties advocated a separate republic of the Rhine, who years ago cried out, "Berlin will never again be Germany's capital!"? Is he waiting, like a bride, to be forced into it, and later will he draw on white gloves, like Brockdorf-Rantzau at Versailles, when he signs on the dotted line? Are we facing a second Versailles? When we listen to Springer, our most powerful newspaper magnate, it seems that we are.

We the Germans have expected, ever since the end of the war *we lost,* that the Western allies would set our freedom above their own national interests. We took this for granted, for we had been told repeatedly that the last war was won "in the cause of freedom." This implied that the fight would never end so long as there was one corner of the world not yet free, whoever its people were. There was no limit set by common sense. Perhaps it would have been better if the slogan had been somewhat longer and a little more precise, if less catchy. Perhaps it should have read: "We, the Americans, the English, the French, the Norwegians, the Greeks, the Dutch, the

Belgians, the Poles, the Russians, etc., are fighting because we have been forced to defend ourselves." This would not have left the Western allies with the burden of responsibility for an infinitely elastic moral concept. The Germans, with their tendency to oversimplified political thinking, are taking advantage of this moral blank check.

Perhaps the most effective move—though unorthodox and painful—would be for Adenauer, after having first notified his allies of his intentions, to begin negotiating directly with Gomulka. By voluntarily and directly handing over to Poland the Eastern territories—which we no longer possess in any case—without fuss and delay, we could save Poland from having to thank Russia for them. We would be treating Poland as an ally and strengthening our own position. Certainly such a move would be a gamble, but it might be highly successful.

There is another gamble we can take, with a good chance of success, so long as we remain the better players. If we have to recognize the German Democratic Republic, we should do so on condition of having an embassy in Berlin and consulates in the Zone, and, most important, freedom to cross the border as is customary throughout the West and is fitting between two sovereign states. In any case, we already have Eastern spies everywhere; a consulate of the GDR in Munich could hardly make much difference. But a consulate of the Federal Republic in Dresden would be a considerable achievement. Russia and Ulbricht say they want us to consider the Eastern Zone as a sovereign state; perhaps we can achieve more by pretending to do so than by playing ostrich?

The wall can grow no higher than it is now. The Russians are notorious gamblers. Why not play poker with them? The stakes are high, but we keep forgetting that we *might* win the game. So much of our trouble is that the West seems to have lost all self-confidence.

Why is it inconceivable that Adenauer would ever go to Warsaw? Because it would take a great man to take such a step, and Adenauer is not a great man. He has proved to be a makeshift—not a bad one, but nothing more. Because he has formed the pattern of life in Germany for the last twelve years, efficient mediocrity has now become the rule. Because he did nothing to eliminate the enormous confusion after Hitler, the confusion has remained. He has done nothing to make people think about the problems whose direct solution is a matter of life or death for Germany. He has in no way prepared the Germans for the cold winds which are beginning to blow, as sooner or later they do in every democracy, and which a democracy must not blame on God or some sinister enemy. Only dictators can leave losses unaccounted for in their final reckoning. Democracies must be prepared to accept their losses openly, as England finally accepted the loss of India, and France is accepting the loss of Algeria. The German tends to shut his eyes to disagreeable facts as though, if he did not see them, they would disappear.

Adenauer's failure is greater than his success because of the legacy he leaves. He has not filled the vacuum left after Hitler, which now can be filled with anything, including the doctrine that democracy does not work. For this is what I hear every day, at my bank, at the restaurant, on the bus, at the gas station, at the university. The "proof" is that Kennedy, the leader of the democracies, is so weak that he wants to pay for Berlin with our Oder-Neisse territories, or by extending recognition to the GDR. There's democracy for you! They can't even get a functioning government together in Bonn, and they call *that* democracy. Here is something I overheard a few days ago at dinner: "With just a few Panzer regiments, we could have shown them [in Berlin] . . ."

The cold wind that has begun to blow through Germany has exposed what I have feared all along: the majority of Germans are still wholly incapable of applying logic to politics.

So, the Germans are dangerous, not because they are worse or more cruel than other nations, but because within themselves they have no deterrent against evil. They worship their God Efficiency above all other gods. The Economic Miracle is their offering to him, and they would have bought it at any price. Once more, they are waiting to be given the answer, to be led—misled? seduced? Again? Most of my generation is keeping quiet. They never want to be involved again. They were involved too often long before they understood what it was all about. They know only too well what they do *not* want, but not what they do want—except for a new car. If Adenauer did something wrong in his political maneuvering over the Oder-Neisse border and the recognition of the GDR—why, let him! He is the man who got us the new car.

Germany never openly declared her political bankruptcy after Hitler's *Götterdämmerung*. She might, by now, have been judged and perhaps acquitted, but instead she is still juggling her accounts.

I love Germany, and I know well the regions behind the Oder-Neisse line; I spent some of the happiest times of my life there: Pomerania, East Prussia, Silesia. I also know exactly what recognition of the GDR means; I have crossed the border too often not to know. I also know what Russian occupation means. I have spent some time in an East German prison (then a Russian *commandatura*) accused of high treason, as good as condemned to death. Day-and-night interrogations in front of a portrait of Stalin are not something I saw in a theater, but my own experiences. They really do sit in the dark and focus a blazing light on your face; they do come every night and wake you at two or three or four in the morning, and keep firing questions and threats at you for hours on end, day after day, night after night.

But the Russians were not the only ones who pointed their pistols at me. The first time it was an SS man; and when, much later, some Poles beat me half to death, I was only paying for some SS man's notion of German racial superiority over the Slavs, as demonstrated in Lemberg. If I placed all those who were dear to me and who were killed on one side, and those who killed them on the other, and if I let myself fill up with hatred for each killer, I would go mad. I cannot forget the dead for the sake of a new car; I can trade in no part of my life for *la dolce vita*; I cannot pretend that certain things never happened, so as not to offend. I have spent half my life thinking of the dead and the tortured, all of them and everything that happened to them, not because

I have a morbid taste for nightmares, but because I want
to bury them forever. I can bury them only after their
fearful, irrevocable silence has told me everything it has
to tell: why so many had to die, why those who killed
them had to kill, who the true murderers were. How I
wish all the Germans had done likewise; that they might
remember, not only snatches here and there, but everything, leaving out nothing for the sake of their own comfort.

We have had time to look backward and forward
and to keep on searching; we have had enough experience to become wise. We should at least have learned
that while we always have a choice, we can never
have it *both* ways. We have a choice, and we must make
our choice. Thus or so. We cannot live by one law today
and another tomorrow, only to return to the first law the
day after. We must learn to have clear political concep-
tions. If we claim the respect of other nations for our
democratic form of government, we must earnestly make
it work, not let it degenerate into a farce. If we wish to
be no longer identified with the murder of six million
Jews, we must do more than pay compensation; we must
see that it is more than merely bad taste to have a Globke
as our Chancellor's closest adviser,* and to pay pensions
so indiscriminately that it smells to heaven to characters

* Hans Globke served as Ministerial Councilor in Hitler's Ministry of
the Interior during the period of "The Final Liquidation of the Jewish
Problem," and was co-author of the official commentaries on Hitler's
"Racial Laws." He was also responsible for the regulation requiring
Jewish passports to be stamped with the letter "J," so that no escape
for the bearers was possible. On one occasion, Globke publicly remarked
of the cases with which he dealt that "they should have chosen their
parents more carefully."

who would be securely behind prison bars anywhere else in the world.

We should realize above all that we may lose our chances overnight. We hold our place among the free nations on credit; we have not yet been put to the test. When the test comes, Germany will be ill equipped to meet it. Our excellent cars, fine new houses, the sausages and hams in the shop windows, the soldiers on the street, all create the illusion of a power and an importance that we do not possess. We might have had the real thing, but only in the way Talleyrand achieved it at Vienna for a France then utterly prostrate. Because Talleyrand knew what he wanted—peace—and worked for it cleverly, consistently, and ruthlessly, he succeeded far beyond anything the real power and importance of France could have allowed him to hope. He was a man of great intellect and force, absolutely fearless for his own person. Germany has never had such a man. That is one reason she cannot freely relinquish the Oder-Neisse territories— she lacks the necessary self-confidence.

Perhaps the main reason East Germany is a prison today is the German régime there. Lacking the self-confidence essential to the conduct of one's own affairs under stress, the Pankow régime bends over backward to please Moscow. In East Germany there was no Tito, no Gomulka, only an Ulbricht, a Hilde Benjamin. It took Russian tanks to crush the Hungarian uprising, but the Berlin wall was built by Germans. Just after the end of the war I talked night after night with Russian soldiers, officers, and political commissars. They all made fun of

German servility. They received the German informers who came to them every day in a baffled silence, completely taken aback; the Russians had hated and feared the Germans, and were prepared for anything except what actually happened. No one bombed the reparations trains pulling out with German property going to Russia, no one shot or even spat at the occupiers. Instead, they obediently switched from one party insignia to another, obediently came and "spilled the beans" about their neighbors, their uncles, fathers, sons. Not all of them— but so many! Even for the Russians, there were too many.

If the Germans had refused to build the wall, the Russians would have had to do so themselves. Could we have expected the East Zone soldiers to risk their lives for a show of inner strength? On the other hand, would Englishmen have built a wall through London?

What is it that makes the German unable to see, unable to take things in with his mind, with his whole person? He is made up of so many separate compartments, each one existing independently. No one has understood this better than Hugo von Hofmannsthal:

> Nothing they do is of a piece. Their left hand does not know what the right hand does, the thoughts of their head know nothing of the thoughts of their heart, their official thoughts are ignorant of their scientific thoughts, their façades are not in agreement with their back stairs, their business has no accord with their temperament, their public with their private life.

And:

> It seems to me as if they might equally well be saying something else, and as if it did not matter whether they

had said one thing or the other. It is as though they were always thinking several things at the same time.

The great danger of the Germans in a world so precariously balanced as ours is not so much something that is positive and identifiable as it is the *lack of anything definite*—except for their faith in the God Efficiency whom they all worship, big business and little business alike. Incidentally, I wonder how much they profited from the spoils of the concentration camps and all forms of slave labor? I wonder?

Whom do I meet these days in Germany who discriminates between good and evil, without that ever-present addendum: "But what of the others? Haven't they done evil too?" Who is there to say, "X is efficient, but he is not *good*." Is there anything that Germans will not do? When one speaks with a Spaniard about his Civil War, his voice is full of sorrow. One can feel that his whole being is affected, upon whichever side he fought. What is there that will penetrate to the core of a German?

There is much good in the German—in most Germans—but it has never been challenged in the way in which his efficiency and his obedience are challenged, day after day. It was up to Adenauer to dethrone the pagan God Efficiency; it was up to him to say, "There are more important things for us Germans today than the latest model automobile," and he should have named those things, clearly and repeatedly. He should not have let the post-Hitler vacuum continue. Adenauer had a unique and never-to-be-repeated opportunity in German history; our human substance was challenged in 1945 and in the few years thereafter, as never before. It was up to us to become the key then, not because we were economically strong, but because we had just been through a monstrous experience.

We muffed that opportunity, and now we face our task with empty hands and minds ill equipped to plow the field destined to bring forth a harvest to be gathered by our children: the children who look upon us with contempt for our failure to answer their questions.

The big bomb has come into being without our help. We pursue it, trying to understand its meaning. It is entirely possible that our world may be totally destroyed within the next twenty years. I can shut my eyes and see it happen. What a brief incident in the life of the great galaxies we shall have been. But why need it come at all? Why should it happen? *Why?*

Because we have forgotten so quickly, in the very shadow of the bomb, to put our lesser affairs in order. After all, that decision to fire the final bomb and blow up everything will be a human decision. And the decision that it may not be necessary to set it off would, after all, also be a human decision. Our problems can no longer be solved by cars and sausages. The Germans, sooner than anyone else, should have learned and understood.

Perhaps they will understand one day. Perhaps they will learn to smile and to feel pity and to cease sidestepping disagreeable necessity. Perhaps they will learn that there is a kind of success not subject to measurement, which must be worked for, suffered for, and fought for, not with guns and production statistics, but with one's whole being.

:V:

DO
WE
GERMANS
FEEL GUILTY?

. . . . .

Zur Nation euch zu bilden, ihr hoffet es, Deutsche,
 vergebens;
Bildet, ihr könnt es, dafür freier zu Menschen euch aus.

In vain do you Germans hope to form yourselves into a
 nation;
Instead, and you can do it, form yourselves more freely
 into human beings.

German National Character
FRIEDRICH VON SCHILLER (1759-1805)

: V :

Do we, *as Germans,* feel guilty?

To speak in such terms is to assume that there is such a thing as innocence, and that we all live by the same set of values. This would mean putting aside all of our twentieth-century knowledge of history, psychology, and other social science—including all we know today of the causes of race hatred. On this problem, Elspeth Huxley said, in a book review:

> Here is a morality without a villain: we are strayed sheep, not wolves, even when we tear each other to pieces for reasons, or emotions rather, that lie deep in the soul, or that contort the Id. Race is a universal scapegoat for our inner deficiencies; the weaker we are, the more we seek to draw comfort from the believed superiority of our group, be it nation, clan, caste, or race.

Insights such as these came to my generation in Germany as part of what happened to our lives, and we soon learned to disregard such terms as "guilt" and "in-

nocence"; they had been used too often as specious
counters in the game of politics and in the manipulation
—so very easy—of national prejudices. Applied to history, or historical processes, or whole nations, these words
represent an emotional rather than a rational response.
He who places himself outside the law is "guilty," regardless of who he is or where he is.

To my headmaster, I was guilty, because the law
said—as it does in South Africa, regarding the Negroes
and Indians—that the Jews are an inferior race and one
must not associate with them. I became guilty when I
said that we were bound to lose the war, even though I
was only applying simple logic to a given problem of material resources in a modern war. But by the rules of the
game of war, such a statement was enough to make me
guilty of being a defeatist in any country. I also became
guilty when I gave bread to a Russian prisoner of war,
and helped him to escape, just as I would have been
guilty in England had I aided a German prisoner to get
away.

What about the guilt of my friends who had not
chosen Hitler but who, at seventeen, were sent to fight
the Russians? The Russians had, like Hitler after all,
more than once declared that they were aiming at world
domination, and were at that time burning and raping
their way through Germany. Am I not guilty, in the most
appalling way, when I plead with the doctor to give
my starving father an injection, in order to save my
mother's sanity and her life? Or does the guilt lie solely
upon those who brought things to this pass? Who is
guilty of the deaths of the children I saw being roasted

to death on the melting asphalt of bombed Dresden and Chemnitz? Two friends of mine were killed when American soldiers kept up their idle target practice at an undefended city, a few hours before the end of the war. Are those soldiers "innocent" or "guilty"? What of the U.S. army captain who shot me from my bicycle as he rode past in his "Lightning," even though he must have recognized me in my dirndl as clearly as I saw him—is he an attempted murderer, or innocent? When Misha, the Russian driver, risked his life to bring food to me in the cellar of the *commandatura*, surely he was innocent; yet, two days later he raped one of my best friends and shot her brother. My stepgrandmother came from Czechoslovakia, where we had many friends murdered by the SS. But a friend of mine who had been in the resistance against the SS and had saved the lives of many Czechs was quartered alive by Czechs in 1945. What had she done? Nothing—she had a German name.

Three days before the end of the war, two SS men were marching fifty or sixty Jewish women prisoners from the nearby camp down the village street where I happened to be standing. The women were to be shot when they reached the nearby wood. I told the women that the Americans were only ten miles away, and gave some of them milk to drink without noticing that one of the guards now stood beside me. Once again I was a swine, a traitor, guilty of helping to defeat Germany. The SS man drew his pistol, shot my dog, then pointed the gun at me. With the coldbloodedness of seventeen I said drily: "You're making a mistake, with the Americans just outside the village." He jumped onto his bicycle,

turned and disappeared, leaving the women to hide in
the barns nearby. Less than half an hour later I was shot
at by the American captain in the "Lightning." I was taking milk into the besieged town, for the two-month-old
baby brother of a friend, whose father, incidentally, was
a Nazi.

During the night of February 6, 1947, one and a
half years after the end of the war, six Poles broke into
the little house where I had rented a room. They were
DP's from an UNRRA camp nearby, deep in Bavaria.
By the law of the time, these men were subject neither
to the laws of Germany nor to those of the occupation
authorities. When they had burgled the house, they beat
us unmercifully with an old silver-handled riding whip
—it had been a gift from the Kaiser to my father. They
all but broke my spine. Why did they do this? One of
them said that the Germans had killed his family and
raped his young sister. I could see from his distorted
face that he spoke the truth. He was only seventeen
or eighteen years old. Dare I be his judge and declare
him "guilty"? The Poles wrecked the room, tore up
all pictures and papers, including a testimonial from the
American hospital chief stating that I "had given of my
efforts far beyond the call of duty, to the rehabilitation
of the DP's" of that same camp from which the six
Poles had come.

For some mysterious reason I have always felt
stronger than the man who pointed a gun at me, the
men who threw the bombs, the headmaster who tried to

destroy me. I felt I understood more than they did, and that at bottom I was far less afraid than they. I had learned that human beings, like animals, are most dangerous when frightened, and they are most frightened when they are away from their accustomed surroundings.

The twentieth century, with all its revelations in the sciences, has left us stranded in a desert where the old means of human orientation fail us. Formerly the founding of empires by war and annexation was considered natural; today it is a crime. Formerly a soldier was not held personally responsible for warlike acts committed in another country—while seeing himself as the defender of his own family at home; today he cannot be considered innocent: he is bound to kill too many children. It is no longer one country against another, it is one half of mankind against the other half. The social sciences, psychology, even biology, tell us that the good, the innocent, the sane, and their opposites, are equally distributed everywhere. We have learned that it is nonsense to speak of "good" and "bad" nations. We have learned that no war will be the last, so long as we go on dividing people into the "guilty" and the "innocent," judging them by effects, not causes.

To deal with issues on the level of guilt and innocence gives us a kind of relief. If a crime has been committed, it follows that there have been victims, who may then be endowed with tragic stature in our memory. To call the murdered six million Jews the tragic victims of a guilty nation enables us to endure the thought of them. To face the truth, to admit that this slaughter was rather the result of an error of judgment, a simple, if glaring, failure of the twentieth century to make use of available knowledge, is too unbearable.

Why?

It makes us inescapably responsible for the future. Every era of new visions and new worlds begins in violence and terror. Mankind resists being expelled into the unknown, out of the familiar world where the concepts of guilt and innocence have their place and meaning, and where one can believe that it was right to go to war for the glory of one's country.

Ask the surviving Germans of my generation. We no longer accept the validity of the terms "guilty" and "innocent." We no longer believe in war, any war, or in the glory of any one country. We would never fight for the territories we have lost in the East. No matter how much I love the valleys of Saxony, the lakes of East Prussia, I would not lift a hand in violence for them. It no longer matters to me whether a German or a Pole plows the fields that once belonged to my father, so long as he is a happy, contented man. Even Communism is to me a passing phase of historical development; it will never rule the whole world, for there is something in the nature of man which will always resist assaults upon his dignity.

Now that the astronaut in his satellite sees the earth looking like a golf ball, even a United Europe begins to seem an old-fashioned, a limited, idea; we must begin to look upon Australia as a neighbor. Germany came too late with its tortured and tormenting effort to become an empire. It had to end in catastrophe.

What we need today is courage, not the courage of

defiance or aggression, but the courage born of faith in oneself. What has sprung from the mind of man must be mastered by the mind of man.

As everyone knows, we can master only what we have understood. This applies to the bomb and its functions, as well as to those handling it. It applies to everything, including us, the Germans.

Will we ever learn to understand ourselves? To do so, we must follow the inexorable way of our century; we must not forget, we must not overlook, we must not even turn away to hide the grimace on our face: we must look full upon the reflection of our own stupidity even though it stings us like an insult to see it.

We are Germans. We are free to accept this as a potential for growth, or to reject it. But first, we must find out who and what we are.

:V I:

HOW
THIS BOOK
CAME
TO BE WRITTEN

. . . . .

'Willst du nicht Artikel schreiben?'—
Lasst's beim Epigramme bleiben.
Kann ich's euch in zehn Zeilen sagen,
was euch verwundert,
warum euch Honorar abjagen
für hundert.

"Write an article," suggests a letter.
Thank you, epigrams suit me far better.
If in ten lines I can say
what makes you wonder,
why should I ask you to pay
for a hundred?

The Economical Poet
CHRISTIAN MORGENSTERN (1871-1914)

: V I :

THIS BOOK began as a collection of notes, some of which first appeared in the London *Sunday Times*. Most of it was written in Paris, and I spoke about my problems in writing it with the men and women I met during the summer of 1961: French, English, Dutch, Irish, Italians, Americans, Poles, and Russians. Our talks sometimes went on far into the night, often until we were dead tired and upset by all our renewed memories.

Soon I came to realize that the world outside of Germany is keenly interested in my generation of Germans: those between the ages of thirty and forty who will be running things in Germany for a while. People of different nationalities now consider it quite natural for a German who happens to speak their language to talk to them about his concerns, to try to explain matters, to tell his own story. Having shared the horrible experiences of the past fifty years, Europeans are learning to trust each other, to discuss, with very great frankness, the problems of their countries.

The notes upon which this little book is based are not directed at the English, the Americans, the French, or even the Germans, in particular. They are not a proclamation, a lecture, or a program; they are the effects of a self-examination which I have carried on since the war, and they are, inevitably, full of flaws.

But then, this little book is meant to be the beginning, not the end, of a discussion. The notes remain notes, the letters from readers have been neither glossed nor analyzed, but simply appended. What was terrible at the time remains terrible here; where no sun shone, no sunshine has been made up; where the generals ran home to hide in their haylofts, they still run in these pages.

Needless to say, not all of them ran. Needless to say, not every German killed a thousand Jews. Nor should anyone ask here, "How did the English treat the Boers? The Spaniards the Aztecs? The Russians the East Prussians? The French the Algerians?" This book is about the Germans.

Neither the *Sunday Times* nor my German publisher, Rowohlt, told me in any way what to write or what to omit. The *Sunday Times* had accepted my articles in principle before a line had been written. Rowohlt had no idea what the finished book would be like when we signed the contract. The telegrams and cables from leading publishers in England and Italy, the phone calls from Paris and New York for publication rights, all followed publication of the first article in the *Sunday Times*.

No one really knows who or what we are, but people everywhere are interested and want to talk with us, so long as we do not pass over something here, forget something there, and so long as we do not try to equate each Jew, each Pole, each Frenchman we killed with a dead Aztec or East Prussian or Dresdener. No brutal death in Theresienstadt will weigh less in the scale because of some brutal death in Lima five hundred years ago. The German mother who searched for days and nights along the frozen Oder River for her lost child, crazed with grief and tormented by the icy blasts, is a sister of the Jewish mother who told her child a fairy tale in the gas chamber until they both were suffocated.

Only by remembering this, by passing over nothing, by refusing to equate statistics with humanity can we speak with our neighbors and hope to be understood. We must begin then, not with the Aztecs, but with Theresienstadt, and end, not necessarily, with my beloved East Prussia. The truth, especially the truth about ourselves, is hard to bear; it is brutal.

The world is waiting to hear this monstrous truth from *us*: not from an embittered emigrant, not from a Jew, not from a former admiral; not in parables and symbols and abstractions, not written on rock, nor on the dissolving clouds. The world expects us to state simply how it really was; the world wants to know what will be, and how we will make it so.

. . .

I am no political writer. I much prefer to write poems about butterflies and lake trout. I never dreamt that
my first book published in Germany would be *this* book.
I was sure it would be a slim volume of poetry. That is
what I wanted, hoped, and dreamed about.

I had wanted to write a comedy, a comedy of errors,
because life is full of errors, of misunderstandings. My
characters were to lose things which would then be
found by others, who would draw the wrong conclusions
from them. When I was thirteen or fourteen, the possibilities of such a plot seemed hilarious.

Life is still full of misunderstandings, and we continue to draw the wrong conclusions when we find things
belonging to other people. But we should not play
Othello and strangle poor Desdemona for a handkerchief.
A handkerchief, a sentence, a chapter—what does it
amount to, considering the whole? I hope this little book
will not be judged entirely by its mistakes.

One reason I came to write about politics, after all,
was that I studied history and discovered the simple
truth that history has no beginning and no end. History
does not date from 1918 or 1933 to 1945, or from 1945 to
1961. It is a great river made up of currents from many
sources. Its tributaries may be muddy or clear; it may
be subject to floods or droughts—all kinds of catastrophes. We may cross over this river on great bridges or in
little cockleshell boats; we may fall in and be carried
away, whirled into the rapids; we may swim in it, let
ourselves be borne along in the sunshine, and play with
the silvery fish. Like silvery fish were the airplanes that

played together in the blue sky; but when they fell, their tails flaming, they were nothing, in the end, but a heap of scrap metal.

This is not poetry, but history. The editors and publishers knew it. They wanted this book, not because they have an axe to grind, but because the fun up there in the blue sky does so often end with the heap of scrap on the ground—and because that is so quickly forgotten. We forget so quickly what happened so quickly.

Do we not forget? People want to know. Requests for the book have come in from Cannes, Strassburg, Mexico City; all over the world people want to know what we, those of us about thirty-five years old, remember of wartime Germany. From the beginning, all those telegrams, calls, letters from near and far, sudden visitors, forced themselves between me and the poems I wanted to write.

Only after I had written this book did I know why I had written it.

:VII:

LETTERS
TO A FRIEND
IN FRANCE

. . . . .

Will no one answer?
Will none answer?
Will no one, not one, answer?

WOLFGANG BORCHET (1921-1947)

:VII:

Dear Tonita,

You say you cannot understand why I have been making myself unhappy for months on end. A morbid affectation? You say, "Look at our friend Alain Cl. . . . T. . . .* He does not think of the concentration camp any more; he thinks of tomorrow. He is much happier than you."

Perhaps he is much happier than I. Indeed I hope so, for his sake. But with me, it is this way: because I think of tomorrow, I must think of the concentration camp too—and I shall keep thinking of it until I receive an answer from all the dead I have seen everywhere. What you do not know—for you are still so gloriously young—is this: the most horrifying things can happen

---

* A French Count taken to a German concentration camp at the age of sixteen.

from one day to the next, if we do not keep an eye on what is going on *beneath* the surface. Because I do not want to see you and your son Alexis hanging from a tree, or crawling out of a Paris transformed into a blazing desert by a single poisonous mushroom—that is why I keep asking the dead why they are dead, and the living, why they killed. A tedious and painful interview.

I am German. What this means is not as clearly definable as being English or French or Spanish. You understand it even less, because there was little in our relationship to remind you of my nationality. We speak English, French, or Spanish with each other, never German, since you do not understand it. We were never in Germany together, and perhaps I never will have a chance to show you the Germany which *is* Germany to me. When I was growing up there, in the eastern part, in the center of Germany, I was called in fun, for no reason which I could discover, "the foreigner." But today I know that if it is possible to be all German, then that is what I was in those days. But I have learned since to reject everything German that prevents me from living as a human being—a humane being. What exactly this means you will know when my last letter reaches you.

I reject everything German that prevents me from thinking and feeling as a European.

There remains everything German which permits me to be a European, and a human being as well. This is a great deal. It is a great potentiality, and it is up to me to bring it into being. I mean that there are great possibilities in being German, but unlike those in being French or English, each German has to discover them for himself, and consciously put them to use. This has to be done, I believe, in a state of inward independence from one's surroundings.

What is called German in general, apart from these possibilities, is mere sound and fury. A real Germany in the sense of a functioning political organism has never yet existed in history. Such a Germany could now be possible only as a gift to Europe, a kind of dowry. As a physical reality, such a state can no longer come into being; a new national state would be an anachronism in modern Europe.

The Story of a Letter to *Time and Tide*

August 15, 1961

Sitting in the waiting room of a London dentist, sometime in August 1954, I picked up a copy of the journal, *Time and Tide*. After idly reading a few pages I came upon an article that greatly disturbed me. It was about Lord Russell's book, *The Scourge of the Swastika*, which the writer of the article felt should never have been published. At the time I believed what I had read in another paper, namely that this publication of the horrors of the Third Reich was being suppressed for political reasons, because it was necessary to make Germany acceptable to the English for membership in NATO.

The moment I was home I sat down and wrote a letter to *Time and Tide*, sent it off, and forgot about it; I had many other things to worry about in those days.

Here is the letter as published in *Time and Tide*, August 28, 1954:

THE SCOURGE OF THE SWASTIKA

Sir: The daily paper this morning contained notice of Lord Russell's resignation because of the attempted banning of his book, *The Scourge of the Swastika*. I saw the notice only by accident, waiting for a friend to ring off at the other end of the wire. I have not been able to do any of the work piled up on my desk since.

With uncanny clarity an incident came back to my mind which occurred many years ago. My father was a surgeon in a town in Saxony and after his call-up many patients on leave dropped in for a chat with my mother. Shortly after the beginning of the war an elderly man in the uniform of an infantry private stood on our doorstep and gave our bell a hesitant ring. His face was pale and drawn and he took a seat with great relief. Soon my mother arrived in the hall and after the usual polite inquiries the man suddenly burst out in tears. He spoke rapidly and with a flat voice. His contingent had been ordered to "finish off" a village in Poland. He himself had been made to take small children by their feet and crash their heads against a brick wall as an expedient way to dispose of them. Any refusal to follow the example of his superior would have caused his own immediate death. The private finished his story and told us that he was due to return to the Russian front the next day. He never went. At dawn his wife found him, hanged. I was about thirteen or fourteen years old. After my eyes had been opened by the old man's visit, no month ever passed when I was not made aware of German actions in occupied countries which were in complete discordance with International Law.

Once I was cutting the corn with a horse-drawn binder. It was the custom to wait a few minutes before mowing the last island in the middle of the field so that roebucks hiding there should have a chance to get clear of the blades. This time a man slowly crawled out of this hiding place, his face covered with the blood of a hare he had just been eating, his hair long and matted, his clothes ragged and filthy. He was a Russian prisoner of war who had escaped certain death in his camp in order to die in the fields. His state "on the run" differed little from that of thousands in captivity. Together with other Germans I watched the female concentration camp wardens on the railway stations in the mornings, black-booted and carrying revolvers and whips, driving along groups of women from every country in Europe—and not only Jews either—chained together. They were starting off on their way to work in a munitions factory.

I could add hundreds of incidents which proved to me beyond all doubt that to a group of my fellow countrymen, human lives meant *nothing at all* and that, for them, in the flush of certain victory, the Conventions of Geneva did not exist. I happened to be in Dresden with my grandfather when that city was bombed, and many children there died a death slower and crueler than any of those who had their heads crashed against the wall in a Polish village, but amidst the hell let loose I could still see the newsreels of the Stukas roaring down on Warsaw, years before.

A few years ago a book was compiled in the American Zone of Germany giving proof beyond doubt of the atrocities committed against Germans living in what was once Austria and then became Czechoslovakia. Women had been quartered in medieval fashion, and burning at the stake came into its own again. American and British journalists helped with the investigations which led to the publication of the book. We all shrink from reading documents disclosing the baseness to which human beings can sink in the wake of a war. But it is far better that we should *know* and be prepared, because otherwise we hoard illusions that might prove costly to our very selves one day.

If Lord Russell's disclosures are true, they should be published at all costs. We must begin to call things by their proper names once again if we want to survive.

I am, etc.,

76 Upper Tollington Park, N4   Gudrun Tempel

Years later I discovered by chance that there had been, on another page of the paper, a brief comment on my letter by Rebecca West:

> I find myself deeply touched by a letter from a German in our correspondence columns this week. The writer manages to convey something of the anguish felt by decent, humane people when they are made a party to unspeakable crimes.

But before I had any idea that my letter might be in print—I had directed it entirely to the editors without a thought of the reading public—and less than a week after

I had mailed it, I received a reply. When I had read it through the fifth or sixth time, I danced for joy through the whole house. Here was an unexpected source of income, from doing what I wanted to do more than anything in the world! Money worries were at the time my greatest worries by far. Here is the letter I received on the Longmans, Green & Co. letterhead:

26th August, 1954

Dear Mr. (*sic*) Tempel:

I have been much impressed by your letter under the heading "The Scourge of the Swastika" in this week's copy of *Time and Tide* and, from all you say, it does seem to me that you might perhaps have the material for a most interesting book on certain aspects of the war from the German point of view.

Your letter is vivid and excellently written. I do not, of course, know whether you have ever considered writing a book, but if the idea appeals to you at all, I should be most happy to talk the suggestion over with you, if you would care to get in touch with me.

Yours sincerely,
John Guest
Literary Adviser

The Age of Tears, or A Book for Ireland

August 18, 1961

At the time I did my best to hide from myself a fact that I knew only too well: this was not the first offer I had received from a publisher. Indeed, I had lived with a similar proposal for years. I had even written several hundred pages—not badly, I think, but in vain, for my manuscript never grew beyond half a book, and half a book does not get printed, unless the author is dead. And I did not want to die for the sake of the book.

Yet, I very nearly *had* died because of that book. I tried to banish that memory; to convince myself, for example, that a lack of money was the reason I had failed to finish *The Age of Tears*—as the book has come to be called. But that is never the real reason for not finishing a book. I wrote this one without having money. The truth was something quite different.

It all began very pleasantly. Living in Ireland, I met a young publisher through his sister, a fellow student. Both were related to William Butler Yeats. His name is Sean O'Hegarty, and he publishes books in Gaelic. He asked me to write a brief autobiography, telling what it had been like to grow up under Hitler and during the war. He asked for a sample chapter and I wrote it in a single day, in English. Sean read it and wrote to me as follows:

April 6, 1951

My dear Gudrun,

I hope it may be convenient for you to meet us tomorrow night as proposed. In the meantime I should like to say that your manuscript seems to me to be likely to be very good indeed, insofar as I can judge from the English translation you were good enough to do. I had hoped when first I mentioned the matter to you that you would be able to write competently, but I felt that the subject matter should, in any event, make up for any lack of sparkle in the writing. The excellence of your style is a most pleasant discovery.

I am glad to say that Séamus ó Néill has agreed to do the translation into the Gaelic. He is an accomplished writer in his own right, having published a successful novel, a collection of short stories, two volumes of poetry and a number of plays, and I understand he has a good knowledge of German. He should be capable of doing a good job. I sent him the German version of your chapter, and when he has translated it into Gaelic I will then put it into English so that you can see whether a fair attempt is being made to adhere to your own style.

As regards the illustrations, I should prefer drawings to photographs. They could be full-page occasionally, if required, but I feel that half-page, in the text, would probably be better. Did you have any success with your inquiries as to drawings from Germany?

I almost forgot to say that I feel that the section in which you explain to your neighbour in Castlebar is rather long and rambling—I feel it comes too much between the reader and your story, which is what he bought the book for!

Sincerely,
[signed in Gaelic] Seán S. ó hÉigeartaigh

A check for thirty-five pounds sterling was enclosed, even though I had asked for no advance, and the matter seemed most satisfactorily settled.

In Ireland I was always well supplied with invitations to spend months at a time with friends in the country. I made myself useful by helping with their horses, or telling stories to pass the time—everyone there has plenty of time. There was, then, no financial problem. Nevertheless, the book did not materialize. To begin with, Sean wanted a German manuscript. The phrase

"Translated from the German" on the title page would heighten the look of authenticity. But I had not spoken or written German for years at that time; I was no longer attuned to the language. Moreover, the sudden shift back to the tongue of my childhood hurled me back into the abyss of that monstrous past and robbed me of the emotional distance conferred by the neutral English language.

At first I tried working on the book at the farm of an old friend, a woman more at home with horses than with people, infinitely kind, and always busy with her plants or animals. She did not interfere with me at all. The place was a writer's paradise, a beautiful old house with a roof that curved like the back of a cow, a cook who guessed my wishes before I was aware of them myself, excellent horses to ride to the nearby sea for a swim, or just for a gallop across those Irish fields—at times to let the warm rain wash my face when it threatened to turn to stone with inner torment.

Sometimes I sat beside a little river, trying to catch trout for supper. I called it Ophelia's river, and I felt rather like Ophelia myself, writing on and on as I did, and understanding less and less the more I wrote. In the end I spent all my time in a greenhouse, eating all the parsnips. As a child I had hated parsnips, but now it seemed that I could not get enough of them. I felt as though I were writing intently all day long, but there was never a line on paper.

All that summer, and the following winter, and the summer after that, I was writing that book, and yet the paper remained blank. Then my money was all gone;

often I walked from one end of Dublin to the other because I could not afford the bus fare. I no longer had anything presentable to wear, so I could not accept my friends' continuing invitations to the country. For a few weeks I found sanctuary with a young painter and his aunt. His father sometimes came home late at night so full of whisky that he shot the locks open when he could not find his keys. In the winter I was freezing. There would have been no one among my friends who could have quite believed me sane.

This was the condition into which I was plunged by a publisher's kind suggestion that I write a book for him, about my childhood in Germany, and in the German language.

A young German couple, Günter and Wilma Petters, literally rescued me from destitution; I am sure they saved not only my sanity but my life. All this happened between 1950 and 1953, while in Germany my former fellow students were busy establishing positions for themselves: on the radio, in the press, in industry, business, politics. They were buying their first cars, building their first homes, having their first and second and third suits made to order. One became a diplomat, another a near-millionaire, a third a government official, and so forth. They had carefully repressed everything I was about to bring to light again with an agonizing effort: the past.

At Günter and Wilma's I began to recover. We took endless walks over the mountains and bogs near Dublin, drank Australian or South African red wine by the gallon, and talked every evening until we fell asleep where we sat, too exhausted to take ourselves off to bed. We did not talk about Germany but about Ireland, and I began to forget again the past I had been searching for. Only now and then was I swept back into the vortex of dark memories, but now I had strength enough to get myself safely back to shore.

Once the Petters's went to Cork for the day. I was just drifting toward my vortex again when I saw a portable typewriter on a window sill, with a fresh sheet of paper in it. I began to write, and here is what I wrote:

BEFORE THE SUICIDE

They ask, and they keep on asking, "Why did you do it? Why?" They do not know what it is like, how it feels, how one thinks, hears, smells, when the great waves come, either with a thundering roar or in silence —black silent waves. Sometimes they are lily-scented and shining green, sometimes they bring a rotten stink with them like decaying trees in the swamp. Then again there is silence, calm; the water feels good, the sea stretches without a ripple to the horizon, supporting the warm gold of the sun. But it is not the calm sea nor the frightening, gaping waves that drive us to do what we must do—it is the great gulf between them, the distance separating them, out there where the others are. With us, in us, they are close together: one moment all is peaceful, the sun shines warm and golden, cooked-lobster-red mouths laugh, everything is brown, a delightfully rich brown—and then the waves come again, howling, pulling and pushing, lifting and pressing, forcing the tension to grow unbearably. If you would only let us run without asking questions! Let us run, leap, fly, and then rest again, when the sea is smooth once more; let us sit or lie in the sun, just so, without questions.

Everything is so much closer to us, everything touches us. We see the branch of a tree, and at the same time we *are* that branch. When someone speaks to us, he touches us. When someone runs with a flag in the street, he touches us; and when our whole body is finally exhausted by all this touching, we go to the moon. And from the moon we look across (not down) at you, the others, you who are like us and yet different from us: you always have coats on, and we are naked. When we make love the lover says, "You are so young, like a child, innocent, trusting, and then you are old, so old, and then young again—but what are you really?" It is like being a rainbow, except that we are the two ends of the rainbow touching the earth in two places distant from each other, with the sea, or a meadow, or a mountain stretching between us. We are in flight and at rest at the same time, big and little at once. We *feel* our own relativity, but you, you others, you only think about yours.

But since you cannot understand us, you cannot help us either. Where you have a good soothing distance, everything is terribly close to us, and if we envy you your distance and go away, as far away as we can, to the moon, then we begin to shiver with the cold. We must burn or freeze or drown, if we want to stay with you.

You do not understand all this? But of course, we know that you do not understand. If you did, you would not keep asking questions, you would not look so helpless when confronted with our inert bodies. How much we wish to be like you, so entirely ourselves—able to push

the wild water and the still water apart, separate flood
and ebb tide, by seven hours, at least a full seven hours—
but sometimes we cannot do it, and then we are seized
with an overwhelming longing to bring about the calm
by means of the storm—the vast, final storm. We dream
then that we have mastered ourselves; we seize the stone
and throw it—at ourselves. Thus we are the storm and
the calm at once, having destroyed ourselves with one
last, wild ride. Then both are inextricably together, the
doing and the being-done-to. We are Christ and his cru-
cifiers at the same time. We have crucified ourselves, because we could not bear it that there should be *both* in
one world.

When my hosts returned late that night, they found
me asleep on the floor.

When I had recovered somewhat, Sean O'Hegarty
sent me another twenty-five pounds. This time I had
asked him for it, because I could see no other way to re-
pay his first advance except by completing the book.

In one of the most beautiful country houses in Ireland, near Dublin, I made a fresh start. This time I really
wrote. I sat myself down in the smallest room in the
house and bolted the door behind me. There was nothing
else I *could* do but write; there weren't even any parsnips.
Fourteen days later I had written one hundred neat pages.
Everyone was satisfied, even the publisher.

Then it happened. I had gone for a stroll in the park,
stroked the soft noses of the cows, asked the gardener to
cut me some late roses—it was getting on toward fall—
changed the water in the dog's bowl. I sat down again

at the typewriter and began again to recall things. Suddenly I felt the ground slip away from under me as though I were on a swing. I wrote on and on, as if my life depended on it.

That night I felt like a devastated town. When I read over the pages I had written, I knew that it was no use going on just then. I had said the same thing over and over again for twelve pages, changing a word here and there sometimes, but sometimes without any variation: The town was burnt, bombed, shot to pieces. It was a dead town. The Russians had taken it, and there was no water to be had except from the water carts. And nobody knew where the water carts came from, and where and when they could be found. I left the house with my two buckets and searched for an hour without finding any. Then I saw two women, also carrying buckets. One of the women wanted to tell me where I would find the water cart—from pity I suppose. The other did not turn around to me and would not talk; she was afraid there would be less water for her if I got some. The two women fell into a silent struggle which took complete possession of their souls. When I could no longer bear to watch them, I turned and walked away.

Today I know that I went away from them because I could understand both of them too well, and wished to spare them the rending conflict. Those many years later, remembering that incident, I was unable to get past it in my writing because I had been engulfed again in that elementary conflict as in a deadly vortex. I could not resolve it.

Once more I gave up, lacking even the courage to

tell my publisher of this fresh failure. I left Ireland, learned to fly an old open plane from which I took aerial photographs, peeled apples for twopence a pound, worked in the fields gathering strawberries and raspberries and plums, and traveled several times to Scotland. I walked through many parts of England and Wales and the Highlands; I never asked for a lift, but I got many. When I happened to have enough money for stamps and tips, I would spend a weekend with friends at their country homes; I never told anyone that I no longer owned anything—I had sold even my camera. One day a friend reminded me that I had now completed my eight semesters at universities in Germany, Ireland, and England. Why did I not take a degree? I began to write my dissertation in bits and pieces. In order to get it done I went into service with a Jewish family in Eaton Square, London, as cook and housemaid, half-days. I did my research at the British Museum and other libraries, walking miles across London to reach them.

Later, an English family offered to finance the final stages of my doctoral requirements. I accepted, and had soon completed the preliminaries. It was at this time I received the letter from Longmans, Green & Company. On the bus going toward my interview with Mr. Guest I thought there probably could be no better time for me.

August 26, 1961

At that time I had another letter in my pocket, that from the German publisher Günter Buchheim, whom I had known since my childhood, and to whom I had sent three stories from Ireland, and the beginnings of

an *Irish Diary*. He offered to publish my manuscript.
This was long before Ireland had become fashionable in
Germany. But I knew that I would want to write about
Ireland much later, when I understood it better. To have
lived there for five years did not seem enough; it was
necessary for me to gain a perspective of it, after the
closeness which had nearly devoured me. To be able to
live in Ireland one has to know much, to have experienced much, for there one does not experience anything;
there, one knows. And so I had packed away my *Irish
Diary* after the first twenty pages.

Today I know that the reason I put it away—despite
the publisher's firm offer and all the advantages of publication—had nothing to do with Ireland.

In writing the *Irish Diary* I had reached a point
where I told about my running away from a great party
in honor of the thoroughbreds on a breeding farm, with a
Hungarian Baron. He was also a refugee and he had lost
all his family. We had both independently reached the
point where we could no longer endure the party, and
took refuge in the stables. We squatted on the feedbox
in the dark and gave ourselves up to infinite sadness. We
were exiled from our homelands, Hungary and East Germany. We considered what we could do. Should we try
to regain what we had lost? Were we deserters? Would it
be simpler to remain here in Ireland, to dance, to work,
to ride horses, to get married and have Irish children?
Who would ever answer that question for us? At twenty-
three one still asks many questions and looks around
for someone to answer them. We left our feedbox, finally,
to return to the party, to whisky and gin, and then back

to Dublin—but not home. Walking down the streets of
Dublin so deep in conversation that we did not notice
where we were going, we suddenly found ourselves in
the slums.

Here I gave a description of the slums of Dublin,
which I knew very well, having lived there too. This may
be the best piece of prose I have ever written. But it was
the end of the manuscript, which stops in the middle of
a sentence. Again I had evaded the decisive conflict: the
many conflicts arising from the problem of *ownership*.
Do the Germans *own* Germany, the Hungarians Hungary? Was it right for the Germans to develop a policy
which allowed them to take Poland away from the Poles?
Is it right, for the Poles, in retaliation, to take Germany
away from the Germans? Generally speaking, does anyone have a right to the land on which he has grown up,
whether or not it has ever "belonged" to him in the narrow sense? But what could we do with such questions in
the slums? They were ruled by a reality and a law of
quite another kind. I forced my way out of these uncer-
tainties by making up an ending for the story. I left the
two of us walking along the canal through the soft Dublin night, in the curiously caressing wind, warm, reassuring, not seeking anything, a wind like the hand of my
nurse. That is, I suppose, where I had fled in my fantasy,
and since a fantasy is something one readily flees to but
does not so easily part from, my Irish manuscript lies
somewhere in some loft. I am sure the publisher has
meanwhile consigned his twenty pages to the waste
basket, as a project without a future.

But in 1954, as I was riding on that red bus to Longmans, Green & Company, I had forgotten all that—or had not remembered it. This time, I promised myself, I would not give up. But I would not try to tell my *own* story as such; that had proved impossible. I would write a novel, disguise myself, by assuming black hair and another name, and thus gain a certain distance from myself. And this time I could write in English—indeed, I was evidently expected to do so. And so I entered his office with the greatest hopes, and a firm plan.

September 1, 1961

Mr. Guest was very kind and told me he had never before written a letter so full of praise to an unknown writer. Then he explained what he had in mind: I was to make it possible for English readers to enter into the soul of a young German who had seen Hitler and the war entirely from within, and of course from the other, the German side. A clear account of my own life was wanted, an autobiography. For this, I would receive an advance on royalties which would enable me to write the entire manuscript. The prospects for such a book were excellent; there was no other like it on the market. Would I try it?

I sat there and felt like a dog who has just had his tail cut off—the tail he had been so ready to wag a moment ago. I knew all too well that I *could not* write the book I was being asked to write. I explained this as best I could, and asked to be allowed to hide behind the thin mask of a fictional character in a novel. Mr. Guest was clearly disappointed, but did not say no. He gave me some excellent advice on stylistic and other matters, and explained the difference between publishing a first novel by an entirely unknown author, and an autobiography dealing with problems of intense current interest. It would be quite impossible to offer an advance on a first novel by an unknown, foreign writer. I understood his reasoning—but I had lost that tail to wag. There had been a firm offer, and now there was nothing except the assurance that the manuscript of a novel by me would be sympathetically considered for publication. Mr. Guest and I had been perfectly frank with each other.

I went home then and began to write my novel. Unlike my Irish manuscript, *The Age of Tears*, I did not know the title of this one until much later: *Antonia and the Fireball*. I wrote steadily, and in order to be able to keep on writing for almost a year, as I had meanwhile taken my degree, I taught girls from all over the world in a convent school. You were one of my pupils, Tonita, as you know. The book progressed slowly, but without special difficulty. I planned to take it to Longmans when I had finished about half of it.

One day I had to give you girls a history lesson about Napoleon, and all of you, being English, French, Dutch, Spanish, Italian, and Portuguese, got into a heated argument, each one insisting that she alone was right, and not listening to the others. One of you called Napoleon a tyrant, a murderer, and hurled other, similar epithets at him, while another declared him to be the greatest genius who ever lived. Finally, the girl with the hand bell passed through the corridor, signaling the end of the lesson which, for a change, you had given me.

That afternoon I was free and went for a walk, still

absorbed in thoughts about Napoleon and your foolish arguments, and, in a deeply related way, my book. Near the nuns' cemetery you caught up with me and ran along beside me without asking permission. After a time, during which I was growing rather annoyed, you began to question me:

"What do you really do, Dr. Tempel?"

Pause.

"You are not really a teacher."

"Why not?"

"Because we noticed."

"What do you mean?"

"You are different from the other teachers."

"I'm sorry to hear that."

"Oh no, just the opposite."

"The opposite?"

"You have to learn everything the same as we do."

Now I *was* annoyed, and knew nothing better to retort than a curt, "Possibly," which happened to be the only true answer. With this I considered the conversation closed, but you began again:

"What, then, do you *really* do?"

In the end, I brought you the manuscript from my room.

The next day I saw you from a distance, sitting near the nuns' cemetery, with the manuscript. You handed it back to me very politely, with many thanks, and in the kind of straight-from-the-shoulder judgment one gets only from children, fools, and sages, you said, "That was nice. And very interesting. But what's the point of it?"

This comment was the death knoll for my third at-

tempt to remember, and write a book about what I remembered. What you had really said, so casually and
ingenuously, was this: "There is no point in merely remembering. Everyone can do that. But it is not enough."

September 6, 1961
This time I told the publisher that I had given up.
I began to write poems, in German and in English,
as a way of shaking off the past.

A good deal had happened since my first abortive
efforts to write in Ireland: I had taken my doctorate,
which had entailed going to Germany for the first time
in seven years, and I had undergone psychoanalysis, out
of curiosity at first, as part of my studies when I was doing psychological research at London University. When
I gave up writing this time it was in a different spirit—
more of a postponement than a defeat. I let matters lead
me as they would, until one day I knew that I must go
back to Germany in order to see *how the others remembered*.

Back in Germany, I soon discovered that *no one* remembered, or wanted to. Their memories were vaguely
drifting bits and pieces. To remember fully was beyond
everyone's strength and desire.

I wrote for the radio and traveled. I spent a summer
in Paris and an autumn in Salzburg, but for the most
part I lived in Munich, in a furnished room near the Isar
River. Once I even went to Spain, just along the south-
ern rim of the Pyrenees; it was there I began once more to
mull over the past. Something in Spain gave me the
necessary courage.

Once the initial curiosity of my German friends about my many years abroad was appeased, they lost interest in me; they did not understand my ways. I was living with no plan, pursuing no career, constantly preoccupied, but with nothing ascertainable. They were all disappointed in me; so much had been expected of me, with all those chances I had had of a decent, that is, a demonstrable, tangible success—all the chances I had dropped one by one! Where were the books for which publishers were waiting? What did I do all day long?

What was I doing? I do not remember on the whole. One day I recall spending in digging up old stuff out of a box—including old poems of mine written on yellowing, shoddy, wartime paper. They testified that during the war I had been a fiery patriot, and a "socialist." Everyone is like that at fourteen or fifteen, when the aggressiveness of puberty causes one to attack everything: money, the "enemy." There were traces of the "lyricism" from some Hitler Youth song. At any rate, I seemed to have been capable, at that time, of feeling thoroughly German. As I knew from my postwar writings, I had not been able to feel so for a long time.

Now I was interested in everything, or nothing; but "being German" did not especially interest me. It did not occupy me particularly; it had ceased complicating and confusing matters. In my efforts to remember, I concerned myself exclusively with the elemental human conflicts that lie far beyond the limits of what is specifically German.

I could not talk about this with anyone in Germany. Few were interested, and they only so far as it might concern them or their work. But it was also hard to discuss these conflicts outside of Germany, for there was no basis of a long, shared experience.

From time to time I still wrote short stories, but when I saw that I could never finish one without at least one death, I gave that up; another blind alley.

September 15, 1961

Toward the end of April 1960, just back from Ireland again, I was on the highway, driving a Sunbeam-Alpine belonging to English friends, when a huge oil truck ahead suddenly swerved. The colossus of steel and rubber surrounded me, above, in front, behind, to the right! While my car was smashing up, I was wrapped up in it. For a few seconds, I died; not for the first time in my life.

What I mean by dying is this: to accept one's death wholly, willingly, when there is nothing—not a second's time, not a hand's breadth—to separate one from it. This, to me, is what it is to die—it happens inside.

In my experience, it is harder to die when the agent —not the cause, which may often be too remote to come under consideration—is another human being. I do not know what it would feel like to face a murderer whose long-intended victim I might be. To me, the killer is always the mere tool of something originating outside himself.

The truck driver, too, "killed" me. He had seen my tiny car coming on, two or three yards behind his behemoth, but all at once the sense of his power—and who

knows what obscure motives, of status or class rivalry—
made him assert his "right of way" against my intention
to "pass him." So he testified at the hearing.

I was not dead, but I was mortally exhausted. I had
experienced this kind of inner death before, but the other
times it had come under exceptional circumstances, of
dictatorship, war, military occupation. Here it had happened in peacetime. While I waited at a Stuttgart gas
station to be picked up by an ambulance, I realized
something that shocked me deeply. Although someone
had nearly succeeded in killing me, when I telephoned
one friend after another in Munich, no one could quite
manage to come to Stuttgart for my sake. In childhood
we often daydream about dying, because to die is, as it
were, our ultimate claim to the compassion of our fellow
men; it confers a right to wholehearted attention as nothing else does. Each time I had felt myself "dying" I
had longed for somebody who would "feel for me," but
circumstances had ruled out such a possibility. This time,
when I awoke from my "death," there were many people
in the vicinity I could call, even close friends. But none
of them had time to come. This meant that, those other
times, it had not been the circumstances that were to
blame, either. It was something quite different: people
are *no longer able to feel* the monstrousness of a death
inflicted by one human being upon another.

As that realization took form in my mind, I felt all
my strength leaving me. Nothing was left to cling to;
I felt utterly alone. If I wanted to survive, I had to survive without any expectation of pity, or interest in my

life and death, without even expecting anyone to recognize my existence. We no longer include the death of others in our experience of life, nor even our own encounters with death.

Through that deadly shock I suffered in Stuttgart —not during, but after the accident—I lost the impediment to finishing my book: my great self-pity for my many deaths and for the many deaths I had seen.

Now I understood that we Germans do not want to remember the past *because* it is so full of death by violence. For if we remembered the past, we would have to understand it, too. To understand it, however, is to know that it was caused by human beings, not by God or fate or chance; not even exclusively by Herr Hitler.

We are not so much *guilty* as *responsible*. Wanting to be pitied for our suffering in innocence, dying in innocence—for we did feel innocent, as in a sense we were— we had to think of those who *caused* it all as *guilty*. I had been unable to finish my books because I could never decide who was guilty and who was innocent, who deserved my pity and who would pity me—often so close to death—for all I had innocently suffered.

The term *guilt* is too mixed up with the past to mean anything now: "It *was* your fault . . ."

But "You *are* responsible" has a definite meaning. This is the new outline people now have in my recollections. It involves continuity, whole lives, and the sum of all human lives. I need wait no longer for someone to pity me. All that dying has suddenly acquired a meaning: it enables me to understand *my* responsibility.

Now I no longer need to feel sorry for myself. Suddenly I no longer have time for that. What had always seemed most pitiable to me, the violent death inflicted by one man on another, has now become bearable, because it is *up to me* to make sense of it, to shoulder the responsibility for it.

:VIII:

MARGINALIA:

Letters from Readers, and How the Book Was Received in Germany

. . . . .

If we had won the war with waving
of flags and roaring, if we had,
then Germany would be past saving,
then Germany would have gone mad.

. . .

If we had won the war, I bet
that heaven would be national,
the clergy would wear epaulets,
God be a German general.

. . .

Then reason would be kept in fetters,
accused and always on the spot.
And wars would come like operettas.
If we had won the last war—but
we were in luck and we did not.

—from *The Other Possibility*
ERICH KÄSTNER (born 1899)

:VIII:

Dear Gudrun Tempel,

I do not know who you are or where you are. But I have just read the first part of a series of articles in the *Sunday Times*, "The Germans."

I am Austrian by birth and lived through the entire Nazi period, including the war, in Berlin (I sent my family to England in 1938, when we lost our citizenship —my wife is Jewish), and have now been a British subject for the last ten years. I am much older than you and I experienced the Nazi period consciously from the start, fought my private war against the Nazis, and followed postwar developments in Germany. I have some of my best friends in Germany, but I am "allergic" to many Germans and Austrians.

That is enough about me. What I read of your article, your first contribution to the *Sunday Times*, has touched me strangely, with a sense of hope, because it comes from one of the younger generation. How much more clearly you see things than the older generation. I look forward to your next installment: "Why Democracy Fails—" I wonder whether you will be putting voice to more of the things which, for a long time, I thought I alone knew.

I agree with almost everything you say. Almost— for in one respect I am of quite a different opinion. You write, at the end of your piece, that you are quite sure the Germans had no idea of the extent and the horror of the persecution. That may be so, but *why* did they have no idea? That is what matters. The German people did not know because they did not *want* to know the full extent of it. They could probably not have prevented it, but no one wanted to know these things, because it is so much easier to live not knowing. I knew about the gas chambers by the end of 1942, because I wanted and needed to be certain of the horror.

Have you ever read Rainer Maria Rilke's *Letters to a Young Woman?* If not, I would gladly send you an excerpt from a letter written in 1919.

This letter is entirely spontaneous—I put the paper down and my pen slid over it as though of its own accord. It is probably quite incoherent.

But do drop me a few lines, if you feel like it—tell me where you live—I sometimes get to Germany and would like very much to know you.

Yours most sincerely,
Paul Rosbaud

Sunday Times,   *November 26, 1961*
Sir,

As a German of roughly her generation, I read Miss Tempel's indictment in the *Sunday Times* with great interest. I am not prepared to accept the *Wir haben es nicht gewusst* legend. She assumes, quite correctly, that the very people "who would not have invited Hitler to their tables" supported him because of his hatred of the Communists.

The first concentration camps were erected by Göring shortly after Hitler's rise to power, to torture and put to death the Communists and Socialists as well as all others who disagreed with Hitler. The existence of the camps was known to everybody in Germany who wanted to know it. The clergy, Gypsies, the Jews, and finally—towards the end of the war—Hitler's original snobbish supporters, followed.

When that began to happen, they made a rather belated attempt to demonstrate their dislike of being with Hitler at the same table by planting a bomb underneath it. Although they convinced themselves and, so it seems, a great number of people that *das heilige Deutschland* was at stake, as Miss Tempel points out very correctly, it never really existed.

Even if we are to believe Miss Tempel that nothing of the mass slaughter did leak through in Germany, the official executions and brutalities that we could see all around us should alone be enough to stop anybody writing "Did-we-or-did-we-not-know" books.

I for one was told by soldiers returning from the

front of the mass killings of people in closed trucks in 1943, and besides every German could see and hear enough to make the revelation of exact details of the brutalities of the war quite unimportant.

Miss Tempel's observations of present-day Germany are accurate.

Helmut Müller

Dublin

(BBC letterhead) *London, November 29, 1961*
Dear Gudrun Tempel,

For the moment, only warmest regards plus congratulations! Your series in the *Sunday Times* is by far the best statement about Germany and the Germans in —ty years.

I hope this letter reaches you. If so, I should be glad to hear from you.

Yours,
Carl Brinitzer

Sunday Times,   *December 3, 1961*
Sir,

As a young, German-speaking officer serving with BAOR in Western Germany, I have read Miss Tempel's picture of modern Germany, and I was interested to see the letters from Herr Müller and "A Refugee," particularly because they seemed to suggest that Germany was slipping back to the *ohne mich* days of the late dictatorship.

To some extent I would agree, but many of the younger and informed West Germans do not want to see a West Germany in which internal politics are so avidly pursued that the rest of Europe is ignored. I have been surprised by the number of young Germans in their late teens and early twenties who are most keen on the idea of West European integration and a common West European political community.

I only hope for all our sakes that the healthier attitudes of young intelligent Germans will prevail in the years ahead, and that the gloomy prognostications of Miss Tempel will not be fulfilled.

Aldershot   (Lieut.) J. S. B. McCord

(Partially printed in the
Sunday Times of December 3, 1961)

November 27, 1961

To the Editor of the *Sunday Times*,
Re: "The Germans—an Indictment of my People."

Sir,

Although Miss Tempel speaks comparatively well of the German Navy, I am not at all in agreement with her wholesale condemnation of our people. She is right inasmuch as quite a number of us might be better prepared to meet the cold wind of the Cold War, but which Western nation is fully prepared in this respect?

Quite obviously she has only a very incomplete perception of the difficulties of rebuilding political thinking in a nation whose leading class was decimated three times in thirty years, and which suffered frightful losses among its possible political leaders.

I welcome criticism, but it should be founded on knowledge. This is sadly lacking in Miss Tempel's two

articles. Her history is rather shaky, her insight into present German life far too narrow and superficial. Evidently,
she knows neither the realistic younger generation nor
any of the great number of Germans who are interested
in politics and not only in cars.

Her articles give the impression that she has been
in contact—and that only for a few weeks—with a small
number of intellectuals of her own age group whose lives
and outlook were badly shattered by war and post-war
conditions. This is not at all sufficient to permit her to
deal with such a difficult, delicate, and many-sided subject. The consequences are sweeping statements and dangerous half-truths. She has created distrust where understanding is needed. . . .

Sincerely yours,
F. Ruge
Vice Admiral (rtd.)
Federal German Navy

Tübingen, Linsenbergstr. 29

Sunday Times,   *December 12, 1961*
Sir,

It is perfectly true, as Lieutenant McCord said in
his letter last Sunday, that Germans in their teens and
twenties today are most keen on the idea of West European integration.

There is very little I can say to the letter of Vice-
Admiral Ruge. He said "knowledge is sadly lacking" (in
me) and my "history is rather shaky." I think I owe it to
my teachers—Professor Schnabel and Professor Maunz
of Munich, and Professor Moody of Dublin—to tell him

that they were kind enough to give me a doctorate in, among other subjects, History and International Law, and this, *magna cum laude.*

He also claims that my "insight into present German life [is] far too narrow and superficial." I must say that I would not like to change mine for his presumably wide one, which led him to advocate German nuclear rearmament and suggest that the Danish Navy should join NATO under his command.

Admiral Ruge was one of Hitler's highest naval officers right to the end of the war. Does he really expect me to feel happy about his telling our politicians what they should do?

Hamburg-Reinbek   Gudrun Tempel

December 12, 1961

Dear Miss Tempel:

Many thanks for sending me, without comment, your creditable academic records, which round out the picture your articles (with photos) conveyed to me. Let me in turn send you herewith the complete text of my letter, recently printed in the *Sunday Times* in abridged form.

However, even the best of academic records are no substitute for sympathetic insight, and no reparation for the harm your articles have done.

Sincerely,

F. Ruge

Vice Admiral (rtd.)

Federal German Navy

Tübingen, Linsenbergstr. 29

December 17, 1961

To the Editor of the *Sunday Times,*

Re: "An Indictment of my People" by Gudrun Tempel (19 and 26 November).

Sir,

I know your lack of space. However, as Miss Tempel has seen fit to take evasive action, I should be much obliged to you if you could publish the following answer which I have condensed as much as possible:

In her answer of December tenth, Miss Tempel has not given a single fact to refute what I said against her wholesale indictment of the German people. Good exams (she sent me her certificates) are not always proof of political perception. In her attacks on me she is wrong on every count. To give one example: According to her, I suggested "that the Danish Navy should join NATO under my command." Three major mistakes: Denmark (with her Navy, of course) has been a member of NATO for 12 years; as a member of our Ministry of Defence I could never hold a NATO command; I always advocated a D a n i s h admiral as commander of the Danish and German naval forces in the Baltic approaches. On the whole, she is as far off the mark as in her assertion "that Germany has no experience in losing things . . . as Russia lost Manchuria." What about the Polish corridor, the province of Posen, Upper Silesia, Alsace-Lorraine, and all the German colonies after World War I?

Miss Tempel's other allegations are equally wrong. I have never advocated German nuclear re(!)armament. (See my contribution to the BBC Radio Link on December 7, 1961.) Promoted to vice-admiral in 1943, I was not at all "one of Hitler's highest naval officers," for even then there were admirals on three levels above me. Moreover, owing to Hitler's disagreeing violently with my views on the situation in 1943, (see Martianssen, *Hitler and his Admirals*, Dutton and Co., New York, 1949), I was given advisory and administrative functions only from that time on. As to "telling our politicians what they should do," Miss Tempel probably refers to the so-called "memorandum" I signed as Deputy Inspector-General of the Armed Forces about 18 months ago. Actually, it was information on military requirements for the Armed Forces, sent to them *with the full knowledge and explicit permission of the Minister of Defence*. In some quarters, "military requirements" was interpreted as "military demands" (which from the context was impossible), which gave an entirely wrong impression, assiduously exploited by negative "friends" of the Armed Forces.

Sincerely yours,
F. Ruge
Vice Admiral (rtd.)
Federal Germany Navy

Tübingen, Linsenbergstr. 29

Moulin de Villiers, France
December 10, 1962

Dear Vice-Admiral Ruge,

Unfortunately your letter of December 17, 1961, had not come to my notice until now. Here is my answer:

: 155 :

1. There was nothing I could have refuted; you did not furnish me with facts.

2. Concerning the Danish Navy and NATO: (a) my point was not that the Danes should join NATO but that they should have come under your command. (b) As you know, your work at the ministry could have been terminated at any time to allow you renewed active service (you afterward retired as Vice-Admiral, not as a civil servant). (c) This is the first and only time I have heard that you advocated a Danish admiral's taking command.

3. Re: "experience in losing things": Was it not to regain the Corridor, Posen, and Upper Silesia that you went to war with Hitler? Thus, we had not experienced *loss* as I meant it: had not accepted it, digested the fact of such a loss.

4. Not "one of Hitler's highest naval officers"? On the one hand you state that Hitler "disagreed violently" with your views in 1943, and on the other hand, after that, you were employed in an "advisory" capacity. . . . Does that make sense to you?

5. "Memorandum": nuclear re (!) armament. Or more precisely—rearmament, to include nuclear weapons. If the purpose of a memorandum made public which states "requirements" of defense is not to demand them, then you must have been failing entirely in your duty. Because if you really thought we "required" them it was your duty to "demand" them, and you should have stuck to that regardless of consequence to popularity, office, all and everything else.

As it is, you try to wriggle out of every responsibility. That is what I said about many (but not all) of "Hitler's highest officers." You seem to be set on proving the point.

Yours sincerely,
Gudrun Tempel

Frau Gudrun Tempel   *Flat C., Easton Court*
Hamburg-Reinbek   *Smith St., London, S.W.3*
           November 12, 1961

Dear Madam,

May I express my admiration for the courage and candour of your articles in the *Sunday Times*—I see the paper irregularly so have not followed the correspondence that appeared after the articles. It gives one new faith in the German people to read the views of anyone of your generation, writing with such realism.

I knew something of Germany in my early youth before the first world war and loved it then, but since the last war, those of us who are concerned about the victims of Nazism in less fortunate countries than our own, have been deeply shocked by the lack of desire to atone for those crimes. Of course considerable sums have been given to Jewish survivors of slave labour and concentration camps, but after all these years, those persecuted for other than "racial" reasons—stateless Poles, Czechs and others—have been denied reparation until quite recently when an agreement between the West German government and the UN High Commissioner for Refugees was made (but not yet enforced) to compensate other categories of victims. The majority of Germans I have met of late years, with some honourable exceptions, feel little responsibility for the past and considerable indifference to the plight of the victims of those horrible crimes. Yet as one knows, many of the noblest Germans opposed the Nazi régime, and in honour of their memory one would hope that a greater proportion of the German people would ensure that they did not die in vain.

There is much to criticize, I know, in other countries, including my own, but at least there are always protests made by groups or the general public when injustice is done. But in Germany, so many ex-criminals remain in high places: judges, doctors of medicine who disgraced their profession, and great industrialists who freely employed slave labour from occupied countries, and who so far have done little to atone for their crimes.

However, it is extremely heartening to read articles such as yours; they give one hope for the future, for in these times, shadowed by the menace of Communism, the West needs unity and a Germany which has repudiated the recent past.

Yours sincerely,
Anne R. Caton

*

A book of the notes from which the *Sunday Times* selected and printed two articles last autumn has since been published in Germany itself under the title "Germany? But where is it?"

I specially requested the publishers to bring it out as a paperback book, at a price below that of a cinema ticket I wanted young people to be able to buy it; I wanted to see if they would be sufficiently interested in the problems of Germany's past and future to risk less than two marks on it.

For the cover I chose a photograph of a Bismarck tower showing the German eagle—but with some of the stones falling out because its upkeep has been neglected. It is at once neutral and, only on close inspection, provocative.

Thus my rather personal and highly critical views of the Germans have been offered to the Germans. About forty thousand copies have been sold, and for two weeks the book was on the non-fiction best-seller list of, strangely enough, only one of the big newspapers. In Germany the book has been both a very great success and an equally significant failure. Fortunately, the success has been where I least expected and most wanted it: with young and very young Germans. Their response has been quite overwhelming. Some not very rich students have bought ten and more copies to give away to friends. What they say in their letters to me, and in long articles in student and school magazines, is this: at long last we get some idea of what it may have been like; at long last, here is an answer that we can believe.

About two hundred of their letters start off with "Thank you very much . . ." Often they continue with "How did you have the courage?" Ever since I began to receive them I have been trying to think of what it might be they thank me for or where any courage comes in. What have I said that could be of use to them, what could I have written that requires courage?

Did I write the book with the view of helping anyone? In all honesty I must say no, I wrote it to help myself—to sort out things in my own mind which had continued to trouble me. I had offered the notes to the *Sunday Times* because I very much wanted the English, or some of the English anyway, to understand how troubled our minds and memories are.

Above all I wanted to speak up for my generation, to show the differences between mine and the previous one by which Germany is still largely judged.

To clarify the difference in at least one aspect, I would like to mention a sweeping but quite accurate statement made in the book and certainly borne out by the response it has elicited. *Our parents feel predominantly German, our children feel and think as Europeans.* To them, many of the problems of their elders seem highly parochial, additional and unnecessary burdens to an already highly complex set of problems concerning their future, and the future of the world. In their letters they thank me for having both dealt with and disposed of the one word that troubles them: GERMANY. Is it something or is it nothing? My answer is, it is both; but it certainly is not what we had always been told it was, or what so many of our elders still want us to believe it is: a sacred institution in the name of which all crimes committed must be excused.

In fact, I say this: Nationalism no longer has a true function in modern society; it has been a protective cloak under which some of the most violent human struggles as well as human achievements have been hidden.

It is now time to forget about it; not throw it away but outgrow nationalism by understanding its basic governing principles and the human needs from which it developed: among them the supreme human need to belong to something, somewhere. This need must be heeded, must be satisfied; it cannot be ignored. And I add: we have to find the answer, examine the possibilities, discover, discard, look again: we must struggle for an answer that will lead us to a new form, and not supplant nationalism by super-nationalism.

The twentieth century has confronted us with immense questions and we must answer them or perish. We must answer them as Germans, too, since that is what we happen to be. We are Germans just as some people are black and others are white; we must neither enlarge nor ignore, but face what we are. All people may be equal but not all people are the same. Communism tries to dispose of the question of diversity, which can never be finally leveled except by total extinction. Diversity is an essential ingredient of life. We must *balance* it anew every day of our lives if we want to survive.

That is the value of that much-used phrase "a world in the balance." From the letters I received I could clearly see that the young people really have understood that this is so: a fact, a reality to be lived with. The generation before mine, which still runs the affairs of this "world in the balance," particularly in Germany, has coined this phrase, but I often wonder if they really understand it. Has its significance penetrated through the many layers of protective preconceptions left over from previous centuries, including the unquestioned and unquestionable moral value attached to *loyalty to the fatherland?* In other words, nationalism is still a part of their lives, but it is no longer accepted by the younger generation as some God-given heirloom of which it would be a crime to dispose, even though great universal happiness could be achieved by disposing of it.

I think that the effect of the discussion of Nazi crimes, as I had witnessed them, and of the part which we all played in their coming into being, was bound to be very different for different generations of Germans. One generation feels too emotionally inhibited to talk about them on nationalistic grounds—one does not soil one's own nest—but the next generation does not consider it important where they took place: *they detest horror regardless of its context.*

Our children know much more about the exact world situation than we do. They feel the horrors of it as if they were rubbing against their own unprotected skin. They are not capable of abstracting these horrors, labeling them, of attaching helmets, swords and colored ribbons to them, or of hiding them in any way. The horrors of our age and times have reached such dimensions that they can no longer be hidden in this way. And it is a plain fact that it is in Germany that the greatest horrors of our time and age—should one say so far?—took place.

The book talks of these horrors. German reaction when it was published has proved to me that a large part of German youth has an intensely deep concern about what happened; pictures of concentration camps reach the very core of their beings because they continually *place themselves in the situation of the victims* of such horrors. For them the identification with THE VICTIM is possible, unavoidable, because the chances of suf-

fering such horrors have increased a thousandfold since
1945, and they cannot see strength enough in their parents to assure them that they will help. They feel—not
always, not day and night, but some days and some
nights—that they and the men, women, and children who
walked into the gas chambers are more or less in the
same boat. The recognition of this is a pain that really
hurts.

But their parents, in essence, forbid them to feel
such pain, to be so concerned. Why? Because most of
them—wittingly or unwittingly—either took part in cre-
ating that terrible world or at least tolerated the creation
of it. Remembering their very personal part in that most
frightening recent history of Germany would bring them
closer to a looming abyss that still waits, uncovered, one
short step away.

They try to comfort their children by saying, "Look
around, not only us, the whole world is rotten to the
core." It is not genuine concern but a terrible glee that
makes German magazines give so much space to gloomy
articles on France's future, "full of OAS fascists or else
disaster," to all the follies and failures around us, to cruelty elsewhere.

In re-enacting their own recent past against a back-
drop of horror painted across a map of the world, they
like to make their roles look very small, very insignificant.

Perhaps the young people of Germany thanked me
because I drew a life-size picture of Germany's horrors,
labeled it Germany's picture, and had our parents and
grandparents take their places in it. I made no attempt
at judgment, I just tried to keep the proportions right.

Those who recognized themselves in the picture felt that they had been hit below the belt. Many reacted violently, but because of fear of public opinion none spoke out. If I had had a job in Germany or attempted any kind of career there, I think the book would have destroyed my chances. As it was, there were people who got up and left the room when they realized who I was. Evidently they did not wish to breathe the same air with me. In a way I preferred them to others who had the means to fight the book above ground but did not: the editors of three of Germany's four national newspapers. One wrote a personal and poisonous letter to my publisher, but none used their papers to air their views, for fear of what would be said abroad. All of these editors had been active journalists in Nazi Germany, and that onus forces them to keep quiet—a very unfortunate state of affairs. They continue to point out their virtuous articles on Nazi criminals who are brought to court, and in their papers they do applaud the fact that these get punished. But they conveniently forget that they themselves were the soil on which the poisonous mushrooms had a chance to grow. In fact, reading through the list of major German newspaper editors—there are, of course, notable exceptions—is like reading through a *Who's Who* of major and minor Nazi journalism. One would not necessarily suspect this from what they write; maybe some of them have had a genuine change of heart—why not? But it is much more interesting to see what they *do not* print, and, in both directions, the smugness with which they make their selections. They have good reason to feel safe; they are among their own kind and who, sitting

in a glass house, will throw a stone? Before I wrote the
book I thought that this might be the case; now I know
that it is.

Of the few people whom I did manage to corner
and ask exactly what made them hate the book so much
—not those who criticized it, but those who just plain
hated it: an emotion, not reason—not one ever brought
up a single definite argument against it. All they said
was that it should never, never have been published and
that it would do no end of harm to the German's image
in other countries, just when we were beginning to be
trusted again. In fact, one of my publisher's representatives abroad fought the book which he was supposed to
sell. To his honor I must add that when I asked him
about it he did give this explanation for his action: he
sincerely believed that the book would distort the image
of the German as he would like it to be seen abroad.

Many prominent Germans have some rather child-
ish ideas about the way in which other countries see us.
Lacking terribly in self-confidence, one of the most serious German diseases, the German tends to feel unfairly
treated whatever happens. He feels he is watched all the
time by some sinister eye. He pays undue attention to
what is said about him and attaches importance to
things so little they would make you laugh. On the other
hand he has illusions about his real popularity. In short,
he takes superficial signs for much more than they mean.
He feels that with a book that is self-critical I am destroying the bud of sympathy that may by now have developed. He scolds me for stirring up a subject—the years
between 1933 and 1945—which he is foolish enough to

believe already has been forgotten everywhere. He cannot believe that no books are more eagerly awaited, more sincerely wished for, than those *by Germans about Germany* during those years. He thinks that it is on a wave of anti-German feeling and manipulation that the book is published in so many countries by so many prominent publishers. He refuses to believe what scores of foreigners have already said and written: that this book—however great its many shortcomings, and small its few merits —if only by its attempt at honesty, has given others, for the first time since the war, a chance to like Germany again, *because it was written by a German.* Their letters have made me far happier than I can say.

Other letters, which not only surprised me but deeply touched me, were from former members of the SS. They had joined it as very young men full of idealism and had been stunned to a dead silence when they came to realize how much they had been betrayed. The fate of these few individual cases has been truly tragic. On the other hand, the dilemma of the newspaper editors is merely the eternal one of the opportunist who lets his flag wave in whatever wind blows. Public opinion abroad prevented the editors from giving vent to their anger at finding themselves portrayed in the huge Nazi canvas. They know they are safe from public opinion in Germany: naturally, it must be on their side with so many Germans facing similar dilemmas. If they could have, they would have prevented publication of the book. Since they were taken by surprise, they now try to drown it in silence, not even printing the usual notice that a copy has been received.

They continue to hate in private, where they can rely on a kind of "old-school-tie" atmosphere prevailing. This must not be mistaken for a Nazi revival. Although they know that they all once wore the same arm band, the older Germans try to ignore the question of the universal German acceptance of Nazism. Because literally millions of Germans supported Nazism in one form or another, conscious of what they were doing or not, violent anti-Nazism has never been popular in Germany and never will be. The person who is strongly anti-Nazi in outlook remains definitely the misfit, particularly in the company of a generation of Germans which has never really understood what Nazism was all about, and which does not want to find out about it now. Yet the very same "misfit" will be welcomed by a younger generation of Germans who want to know, and who only rarely can obtain a full answer from their parents.

What often is called a "Nazi revival," then, by non-Germans is usually nothing more than that "old-school-tie" spirit, of helping each other to get jobs, to build careers, to stay in office. It would be silly to expect the Germans—with no strong feeling of anti-Nazism—to denounce persons in their midst who were the same as they. It is just "not done" in Germany to call anyone a Nazi; where would you stop, where would you draw the line? No, there cannot be the same strong anti-Nazi feeling in Germany as there is elsewhere; it is impossible to the limited powers of human nature.

Who should run the administration of Germany, the law courts, the hospitals, the newspapers, if not the large majority of Germans who, whether they like to be reminded of it or not, at one time supported Nazism? Outsiders must remember that there is no one else available. The few genuine anti-Nazis who could have taken over after 1945 were killed by Hitler; he was a thorough man. It is a fact that there are no anti-Nazis available to replace the others, and, as the excuse goes, the work must be done by someone.

The distressing part of this observation is: all the revelations about concentration camps and Nazi horrors have not been enough to change the German's feeling into definite anti-Nazism. He remains uncommitted either way. His feelings are very mixed and his emotions troubled, but he prefers this uncommitted state. He enjoys the comfort of belonging to the multitude, even when it means having worn the arm band to which, unfortunately, foreigners have taken such an aversion. To him, concentration camps and the arm band do not necessarily go together; to him, it is a downright lie to say they do. In Germany itself Nazism has never been assessed as it has been assessed abroad, for the very simple reason that almost every German was in some way caught up in it. All the discussions, some of the very admirable books by foreigners and emigrants, all the films and television serials trying to analyze Nazism, have been fringe successes, not successes with the vast majority.

It must also be remembered that the faces did not, could not, change very much in German cultural life. The same man who published the racial laws and their commentaries—laws that were, in the very beginning, much more lenient than those of South Africa today— runs his distinguished publishing firm this year as he will next year and the one after. Most of our theaters and opera houses are run by the same people who ran them under Hitler; though perhaps not really Nazis, they never have been anti-Nazis, either.

Perhaps the comment of a friend after the first night, in a German theater, of Max Frisch's play about anti-Semitism, *Andorra*, puts it in a nutshell. I asked, "Did you like it?" After some thought she replied, "Yes, but I felt quite sick thinking about that Andorraner who produced it and must be feeling perfectly smug about it all."

Our cultural life and our Foreign Office and our newspapers are *bound* to be run today by the very people who, for twelve long and very eventful years, said "Heil Hitler" every day, who felt proud to be singled out by the Führer, who wrote long articles—that would make you shake your head sadly in disbelief if you read them today—now ask over and over, "How could it have been possible?" Perhaps we should rather ask, "How could it be otherwise?" They were not Nazis then and are not Nazis now, but *they were not anti-Nazis then and are not anti-Nazis now*.

That is all. The reception which *The Germans* had in Germany bore out what I said in the book. And feeling about it was not divided along social class lines; hatred or liking could be found in all classes. From artisan to duke, all their reactions were spontaneous, whether of gratitude or of hatred. And whatever the older generation of Germans does to prevent the discussion of our past, the younger generation badly wants it discussed. Fortunately, that is the generation that will run the affairs of Germany tomorrow. Every single one of the older generation—the editors who tried to silence the book, the people who went out of the room, the university professor who told me I was a bloody liar, my own sister who thought me completely lacking in competence, every one of those people who tried to convince me that there would not be one student interested in such a book—was once seen—well, shall we say—with a band on the arm? Their desire and the desire of the present ruling generation to keep secret the link between the band and the hangmen is understandable. They would not realize then, as they will not acknowledge now, that a close link did exist between the two. So they do not see, as the English and American and French see, why they should purge Germany of Nazism—the true meaning of which they never understood. My book does not reach them, it only annoys them intensely, it "hits them below the belt." Most of them avoided seeing me or entering into any form of discussion with me.

Anti-Nazism, a set of principles which condemns the ways and means of Nazism outright under all circumstances, would have needed to be a universal and strongly emotional response: an uprising of one half of Germany against the other half, once the cards were laid on the table in 1945. But, first of all, in those days this would have meant siding with the enemy, and, second, there just never was one half distinctly anti-Nazi; the few Germans who were had been executed.

To sum up: the book's effect in Germany shows that a large proportion of Germans are not exactly Nazis but are unwilling to commit themselves definitely against

Nazism for fear of losing the protection of their fellows and, worse, fear of being branded as Communist. For a German to feel anti-Nazi on purely humanitarian grounds is impossible; the idea that one might feel sorry he finds fantastic. When I gave this as one of the reasons for having written the book I was greeted with cynical laughter that made me feel dead cold. Twelve years of Hitler's rule succeeded in undermining respect for human life and happiness and dignity, and established a more pagan outlook that excluded compassion. It has been frightening for me to realize that I have no means of communicating with these people. I feel I have failed with them completely.

Others of the older generation, badge-bearers included, had already begun to think about their role in Nazi society but, because of a terrible sense of loneliness, had not been able to make up their minds. To them the book came as a relief and they said so in many letters. They feel they no longer need be misfits in their natural and genuine concern for the victims of the holocaust—our own Germans included. They recognized the picture I drew from memory; it was their story, too. They did not worry about what foreigners would say about it; they felt the matter was too important to worry about that at all.

Never in the history of my German publisher's firm has any book received so many serious and detailed letters—hundreds of them, and most of them from young Germans. They are passionately interested in what happened, what happens, and what will happen. They are not at all interested in whether or not a man has worn an arm band: that is a quibble to them. They are interested in the man himself, in his sense of responsibility, in his decisions. If they refuse to listen to their elders it is not because they are not interested, but because they refuse to listen any longer to the myth of a huge machine that ticked all on its own. They think men were responsible for it, and that their fathers were among those men. They would like to know how a situation similar to that of 1933 would be faced today. My book gave them one possible answer—not a reassuring one, but one that called upon *them* to make it different. In their letters, at least, they have responded to the challenge; at least some of them have thoughts and feelings that are definite. Enough, anyway, to leave me with three large boxes full of their letters, something which I now have this opportunity to thank them for. I, too, needed to know that I was not altogether a misfit in Germany, in my own country.

ABOUT THE AUTHOR

GUDRUN TEMPEL was born in 1926 in Chemnitz, Saxony. Under Hitler she was expelled from secondary school for "pacifist agitation and exerting a negative influence on her fellow students," despite an excellent school record and championship status in such sports as skiing, fencing, and riding, all of which would have made her a highly valued Nazi youth leader—if she had been willing. At the war's end, she cooked for Russian troops, was stripped of all possessions, spent some time in a Russian prison under threat of execution, and illegally crossed the border many times to be with the scattered members of her family. Miss Tempel began to finance her academic studies by taking on a variety of jobs, first in Munich, then in Dublin. She lived in England and Ireland from 1951 to 1956, and traveled extensively through Western Europe thereafter. In 1953 she worked for a research project on the relation between interest and intelligence in children, at London University. In 1953-4 she obtained her Ph.D. in Munich. Miss Tempel has written for educational radio broadcasts and done translations for UNESCO; in 1959 she published a volume of verse in Ireland, *The Bird That Flew Away*. She began to gather notes for her book on the experiences of her generation in Germany in 1958. She has two more books in preparation, one entitled *Children of Divorce*. Dr. Tempel is, at the present, living in France.